Access to History

General Editor: Keith Randell

Habsburgs and Hohenzollerns 1713–1786

Walter Oppenheim

Hodder & Stoughton

LONDON SYDNEY AUCKLAND

The cover illustration is a portrait of Frederick the Great by Anton Graff, 1782. Reproduced by permission of the Verwaltung der Staatlichen Schlosser und Garten Schloss Charlottenburg, Berlin.

Some other titles in the series:

Europe and the Enlightened Despots
Walter Oppenheim   ISBN 0 340 53559 8

Spain: Rise and Decline 1474–1643
Jill Kilsby   ISBN 0 340 51807 3

From Revolt to Independence: The Netherlands 1550–1650
Martyn Rady   ISBN 0 340 51803 0

Russia, Poland and the Ottoman Empire 1725–1800
Andrina Stiles   ISBN 0 340 53334 X

France in Revolution
Duncan Townson   ISBN 0 340 53494 X

The Unification of Italy 1815–70
Andrina Stiles   ISBN 0 340 51809 X

The Unification of Germany 1815–90
Andrina Stiles   ISBN 0 340 51810 3

British Library Cataloguing in Publication Data

Oppenheim, Walter
    Habsburgs and Hohenzollerns 1713–1786. –
    (Access to History Series)
    I. Title II. Series
    943.6

ISBN 0 340 55045 7

First published 1993

Typeset by Wearset, Boldon, Tyne and Wear
Printed in Great Britain for the educational publishing division of Hodder & Stoughton Ltd, Mill Road, Dunton Green, Sevenoaks, Kent by Page Bros (Norwich) Ltd

Contents

Preface   vi

CHAPTER 1   Introduction: The Habsburgs and the Hohenzollerns   1
   1   Germany in the Eighteenth Century   1
   2   The Empire in 1713   3
   3   The Rise of the Hohenzollerns   5
   4   The Struggle for Supremacy   6
     a)   The Responsibility of Charles VI   6
     b)   The Achievements of Frederick William I   7
     c)   The Causes of the Wars   7
     d)   The Prussian Victory   7
     e)   The Work of Maria Theresa   7
     f)   The Work of Frederick II   7
   Study Guides   8

CHAPTER 2   The Reign of Charles VI   9
   1   The Strength of the State   9
   2   The Legacy of the Past   10
   3   The Creation of the Danubian Empire   11
   4   The Accession of Charles VI   14
   5   Domestic Policy   14
     a)   The Court   15
     b)   The Multi-national Empire   15
     c)   The Multi-religious Empire   16
     d)   Central Government   18
     e)   Finances   20
     f)   The Economy   21
     g)   Local Government   22
     h)   Conclusion   23
   6   The Problem of the Succession   24
   7   Foreign Policy   26
   8   Assessment   28
     a)   The Death of Charles VI   28
     b)   Conclusion   28
   Study Guides   29

CHAPTER 3   Frederick William I   31
   1   The Early Years   31
   2   Frederick William's Philosophy   34
   3   The Army   34
     a)   Military Reforms   34
     b)   The Nobles and the Army   37

c) How Effective were Frederick William's
    Reforms of the Army?   38
4 Foreign Policy   40
   a) Peaceful Policies   40
   b) How Successful was Frederick William's
      Foreign Policy?   41
5 The Reform of Government   42
6 Finances   44
7 Religion and Population   45
8 Education   46
9 The Economy   47
10 Assessment   48
Study Guides   50

CHAPTER 4   Habsburgs versus Hohenzollerns   55
1 The Outbreak of War   55
   a) The Decision to Attack   55
   b) Austria's Weakness   58
2 The First Silesian War   58
   a) The Battle of Mollwitz   58
   b) The Intervention of France   59
3 The War of Austrian Succession   60
4 The Treaty of Aix-la-Chapelle   63
5 The Diplomatic Revolution   64
   a) Maria Theresa's Aims   64
   b) The Rise of Kaunitz   65
   c) Frederick's Policies   66
   d) The Switch of Alliances   67
   e) The Prussian Conquest of Saxony   69
6 The Alliance against Prussia   70
7 The First Year of the War   72
8 The Campaign of 1758   73
9 The Campaign of 1759   74
10 The Campaigns of 1760–2   76
11 The End of the War   77
   a) The Treaty of Hubertusburg   77
   b) The Effects of the War   78
   c) Why did Prussia Survive?   80
Study Guides   82

CHAPTER 5   Maria Theresa   87
1 Austria in 1740   87
2 The Reform of Government   89
   a) Central Government   89
   b) Local Government   90

Contents v

3 Tax Reform 91
4 Reform of the Army 93
5 The Problem of Serfdom 95
6 Religion 96
7 Maria Theresa and her Family 99
8 Assessment 101
Study Guides 103

CHAPTER 6 The Reign of Frederick II 106
1 Prussia as a Great Power 106
2 Law Reform 106
3 The System of Government 108
4 Financial Policies 110
5 Economic Policies 111
6 Social Policies 113
7 The Nobles and Peasantry 114
8 The Army and the State 116
9 Frederick and his Successors 119
10 Conclusion 121
Study Guides 125

CHAPTER 7 Austria and Prussia after 1763 128
1 Prussian and Austrian Foreign Policy Aims in 1763 128
2 The Prusso-Russian Alliance 130
3 The First Partition of Poland 131
4 The War of Bavarian Succession 133
5 The Switch of Alliances 136
6 The League of Princes, 1785 137
7 The Austrian Achievement 138
    a) The Survival of a Great Power 138
    b) The Making of the Austrian State 139
8 The Prussian Achievement 141
9 Habsburg-Hohenzollern Rivalry and Europe 142
Study Guides 143

Chronological Table 145

Further Reading 149

Index 152

Preface

To the general reader

Although the *Access to History* series has been designed with the needs of students studying the subject at higher examination levels very much in mind, it also has a great deal to offer the general reader. The main body of the text (i.e. ignoring the Study Guides at the ends of chapters) forms a readable and yet stimulating survey of a coherent topic as studied by historians. However, each author's aim has not merely been to provide a clear explanation of what happened in the past (to interest and inform): it has also been assumed that most readers wish to be stimulated into thinking further about the topic and to form opinions of their own about the significance of the events that are described and discussed (to be challenged). Thus, although no prior knowledge of the topic is expected on the reader's part, she or he is treated as an intelligent and thinking person throughout. The author tends to share ideas and possibilities with the reader, rather than passing on numbers of so-called 'historical truths'.

To the student reader

There are many ways in which the series can be used by students studying History at a higher level. It will, therefore, be worthwhile thinking about your own study strategy before you start your work on this book. Obviously, your strategy will vary depending on the aim you have in mind, and the time for study that is available to you.

If, for example, you want to acquire a general overview of the topic in the shortest possible time, the following approach will probably be the most effective:

1   Read chapter 1 and think about its contents.
2   Read the 'Making notes' section at the end of chapter 2 and decide whether it is necessary for you to read this chapter.
3   If it is, read the chapter, stopping at each heading or * to note down the main points that have been made.
4   Repeat stage 2 (and stage 3 where appropriate) for all the other chapters.

If, however, your aim is to gain a thorough grasp of the topic, taking however much time is necessary to do so, you may benefit from carrying out the same procedure with each chapter, as follows:

1   Read the chapter as fast as you can, and preferably at one sitting.
2   Study the flow diagram at the end of the chapter, ensuring that you understand the general 'shape' of what you have just read.

3   Read the 'Making notes' section (and the 'Answering essay questions' section, if there is one) and decide what further work you need to do on the chapter. In particularly important sections of the book this will involve reading the chapter a second time and stopping at each heading and * to think about (and to write a summary of) what you have just read.

4   Attempt the 'Source-based questions' section. It will sometimes be sufficient to think through your answers, but additional understanding will often be gained by forcing yourself to write them down.

When you have finished the main chapters of the book, study the 'Further Reading' section and decide what additional reading (if any) you will do on the topic.

This book has been designed to help make your studies both enjoyable and successful. If you can think of ways in which this could have been done more effectively, please write to tell me. In the meantime, I hope that you will gain greatly from your study of History.

Keith Randell

Acknowledgements

The publishers would like to thank the following for permission to reproduce copyright material in this volume:

Cassell Plc for the extract from *Absolutism and Enlightenment*, R Harris (1975); Longman Group UK for the extracts from *Enlightened Despotism*, S Andrews (1968), *A History of Prussia*, R Koch (1978), *Frederick the Great*, GP Gooch (1974); Routledge for the extract from *Frederick the Great*, C Duffy (1988); Weidenfeld and Nicolson for the extracts from *Prince Eugen of Savoy*, N Henderson (1964), *Frederick the Great*, A Palmer (1974).

The publishers would also like to thank the following for permission to reproduce illustrations:

Cover – 'Frederick the Great' by Anton Graff, 1782. Reproduced by permission of the Verwaltung der Staatlichen Schlosser und Garten Schloss Charlottenburg, Berlin.
Bildarchiv der Osterreichischen Nationalbibliothek, Vienna p. 17
Bildarchiv Preussicher Kulturbesitz, Berlin p. 32
Kunsthistoriches Museum, Vienna p. 100
Archiv fur Kunst und Geschichte, Berlin p. 121

CHAPTER 1

Introduction: The Habsburgs and the Hohenzollerns

1 Germany in the Eighteenth Century

Germany as we know it today is a recent creation. Two hundred years ago the idea that most Germans could live together in a single state was unheard of. The people who lived in the area we now know as Germany may have spoken German and been conscious of a shared culture, but they had no conception that a German state might be possible. Instead of one country there existed a remarkable survival from the middle ages, the Holy Roman Empire (see the map on page 2). This had been founded by the Emperor Charlemagne in 800 AD. During the middle ages the Emperor had exercised real power over his subjects, but by 1700 he was essentially a figurehead. Real power had slipped into the hands of the individual rulers of the separate states which made up the Empire.

There were well over 300 of these separate and independent states in the Empire. In addition there were 51 Free Cities which governed themselves and about 1,500 Free Knights who owned individual villages. All of the states, large and small, could pass their own laws, mint their own coins, levy their own taxes, raise their own armies – and, of course, fight each other. This medieval anachronism survived while rulers in much of the rest of Europe were busy establishing large centralised states with well-equipped armies. It would appear that by failing to make similar reforms, the Empire was bound to face conquest by its more powerful European neighbours. But, contrary to most expectations, it survived until 1806.

The Empire's survival appears all the more surprising when one considers how little power the Emperor enjoyed. The Empire was still governed along the lines established in the middle ages. An Emperor was elected for life. A small number of the states (seven in the sixteenth century, rising to nine by 1700) held the title of Elector, and it was these Electors who chose a new Emperor. In theory the rulers of these states could elect any of their number to be their Emperor. In practice the election was almost a formality, since with just one exception since 1437, the Electors had always chosen the same candidate – the ruler of Austria. A glance at the map will show that Austria was the largest state in the Empire and also controlled extensive lands outside its boundaries. The family which ruled Austria was the Habsburgs. Strictly speaking their lands should be termed the Habsburg Empire since Austria was in fact only a small part of the territory they governed, but

The Holy Roman Empire in 1714

it is acceptable to describe the lands as the Austrian Empire.

The rise of the Habsburgs had largely been the result of a series of fortunate marriage alliances in the fifteenth and sixteenth centuries. Despite the substantial lands acquired as a result, the Austrian Empire was never as powerful as it appeared. The Emperor's subjects spoke a variety of languages, practised different religions and each province had its own laws and customs. Nevertheless, for several centuries, the unmatched size and resources of the Austrian Empire meant that no other German state could consider challenging Habsburg power. However, non-German states were another matter. Germany, with its myriad of small states, was frequently the victim of aggression from ambitious neighbours. The disastrous Thirty Years War (1618–48) is the best-known example of the European powers using Germany as their battlefield.

The Habsburgs were obliged to rely on Austrian resources to defend their interests within the Holy Roman Empire. This reliance on Austrian rather than Imperial power was hardly surprising. In reality, the Holy Roman Empire offered its Emperor neither power, income, an army, a civil service nor a government. The title Holy Roman Emperor was, of course, prestigious. It inferred a link going back not just to

Charlemagne, but to the Roman Empire itself. In practical terms, however, it was a meaningless honour. The Holy Roman Emperor raised no taxes. There was an Imperial Diet, or Assembly, which met regularly. It comprised three Assemblies, one for the Electors, one for the Princes and one for the Free Towns. Since each of the Assemblies had to vote in favour for a law to be passed – and in some cases the vote had to be unanimous in each Assembly – it is not surprising that few Imperial Laws were ever passed.

Even if a law were passed, there were no ministers or civil servants to enforce it. The separate states were jealous of their own rights and resisted any attempts by the Empire to restrict their freedom. The Diet could, and sometimes did, vote to create an Imperial army to resist a particular foreign invasion. However, even when they were faced with serious threats from abroad, individual states were reluctant to let their best men go to an Imperial army which might be used by an aggressive emperor for his own purposes. As a result, the Imperial army was lacking in numbers, equipment and leadership. It was far less effective than the armies of the individual states. An Imperial legal system did exist, with courts which dealt with disputes between different states, or petitions from citizens against their rulers. But it was complex and slow and, as a result, the courts were overloaded with cases to deal with. It was quite common for the Imperial courts to take a century or more to make a final ruling in a case, so in the field of justice as in so many other areas, the Holy Roman Empire was not taken seriously.

It is not surprising that the Empire, with its non-existent government, ponderously slow legal system, powerless Emperor and a Diet that spent months debating trivial details, was the laughing stock of Europe. Voltaire, the famous French writer, summed it up when he described it as 'Neither Holy, nor Roman, nor an Empire'. This famous epigram not only highlights the contempt which the Empire was held in, but also that it is much easier to say what the Empire *was not* than what it was.

2 The Empire in 1713

During the latter part of the seventeenth century, the main threat to Austrian hegemony had appeared to come from outside the Holy Roman Empire. The ambitious and aggressive Louis XIV of France (1643–1715) ruled a powerful and united state whose population exceeded that of the whole Empire. From 1673 onwards Austria and France jockeyed for influence and power in Germany, using subsidies (a polite word to describe bribes) to gain allies amongst the smaller German states, and fighting wars against each other from time to time. For many years it seemed as if French power would prevail, and Louis was able to annex some substantial lands, including most of Alsace. By the 1680s French bribes meant that Louis controlled the votes of more than half the Electors. Louis, who had already stood unsuccesfully for election as Holy Roman Emperor against the Habsburg Leopold I in 1658, could now look forward to his candidature succeding when Leopold died. The willingness of German states to accept French bribes is eloquent testimony to the lack of any sense of German identity at this time. However, Louis' hopes of taking control of the Empire came to nothing. Repeated acts of aggression alarmed many of the states, such as Prussia, which in previous decades had happily accepted French subsidies. In the War of the League of Augsburg (1688–97) most German states rallied to the Austrians, and for the first time Louis suffered military defeat.

The climax of Louis' wars came with the War of Spanish Succession (1700–13). Most of the fighting took place in Spain and the Low Countries, but Germany was the scene of one of the decisive battles of the war. Faced once more with a formidable coalition aginst him, Louis had resolved to destroy the threat from Austria by a joint attack with his Bavarian allies. The French plan was destroyed by the mistakes of the French commanders and the genius of John Churchill (later Duke of Marlborough) who led the Anglo-Dutch armies. The Battle of Blenheim (1704) was fought by armies from England, the Netherlands, France, Bavaria, Austria and the Holy Roman Empire itself. This symbolised the Europe-wide nature of the war, and the way in which Germany could be used as a convenient battlefield for foreign armies. The French defeat was decisive for Germany. The French were driven out of the Empire and it meant the end of Louis' dreams of becoming Emperor. When Leopold I died in 1705, his son Joseph I was easily elected as the new Emperor. The peace treaties of Utrecht (1713) and Rastadt (1714) appeared to confirm that Austria was once again the dominant power in Germany.

Austrian domination over Germany appeared to continue undisturbed during the early years of the reign of Louis XV (1715–74) in France. For the first twenty years, Louis showed no inclination to interfere in Germany. Emperor Charles VI (1711–40) was able to concentrate most of his energies on fighting wars in Italy and Spain, and took his control over Germany for granted (see chapter 2). Although it was not yet apparent, there was for the first time for many years the opportunity for a German state to challenge Austrian supremacy in the Empire.

During the years of conflict between France and Austria, four of the larger German states had begun to emerge as independent powers with some influence in European affairs in their own right. In 1697 the Elector of Saxony, Augustus II, had been elected King of Poland. Four years later, Frederick, Elector of Brandenburg, ruler of one of the largest but poorest of the German states, was allowed by Emperor Leopold to change his title from Elector of Brandenburg to the far more prestigious 'King in Prussia' as a reward for helping Austria in the War of Spanish Succession. In 1714 the Elector of Hanover became King of England when Queen Anne, the last Stuart monarch, died without children. In just 17 years, three of the Electors had, more by chance than skill, achieved the status of monarchs and two of them had acquired substantial lands outside the Holy Roman Empire. Meanwhile in the south of Germany, the Electors of Bavaria were consolidating their lands and emerging as powerful enough to threaten Habsburg control in southern Germany. Each of these states, with populations of between one and two million, could now claim to carry some weight in European affairs. The days when the Holy Roman Empire was dominated by Austria and France were coming to an end.

3 The Rise of the Hohenzollerns

Prussia was perhaps the least likely candidate to be the state to challenge Austria successfully. Although a large state by German standards, Prussia was also one of the poorest and most backward in the Empire. It was often referred to as 'the sand-box of Germany' because its soil was notoriously unproductive. Much of the land, comprising forest and marsh, remained uncultivated. Prussia had no natural defences such as mountains or rivers to protect it from foreign invasion, and as a result had found itself frequently playing host to foreign armies during the seventeenth century. Berlin, the capital of the state, was until 1700 little more than a large village with unpaved streets.

The ruling dynasty, the Hohenzollerns, had a long pedigree dating back to 1417 when the family had been awarded the small state of Brandenburg. Over the next 300 years the state slowly expanded, but this was, as with the Habsburgs, more a matter of luck, marriages and inheritances than of any military skill. By 1702 the Hohenzollern lands were made up of six separate states scattered across north Germany – Brandenburg, East Prussia, Cleves, Mark, Ravensburg and Lingen (see the map on page 8). As with the Habsburg domains, these states had all enjoyed their own laws, systems of government, customs and currencies. They ranged from East Prussia where the *Junkers* (nobles) had power of life and death over their serfs, to the small western provinces of Cleves, Mark and Ravensburg, which enjoyed a high standard of living and education and where serfdom had died out centuries before. The only thing these people and provinces shared was that they were ruled by the same person.

With its deep political divisions, low population, geographaical weaknesses, and a monarch, Frederick I (1688–1713) whose main interests lay in spending money on a lavish court, Prussia appeared a most unlikely candidate to be the state which would successfully challenge 250 years of Austrian control of Germany.

4 The Struggle for Supremacy

During the eighteenth century, political affairs within Germany were dominated by the struggle for supremacy between Austria and Prussia. The years 1713 to 1740 were the period of preparation. Whilst Austria under Charles VI continued to take its dominance over Germany for granted and slipped into a genteel decline, Prussia was rapidly growing in strength under the eccentric and single-minded rule of Frederick William I (1713–40).

1740 was the year in which the balance of power changed. The new King of Prussia, Frederick II, launched an unexpected attack on the equally inexperienced new ruler of Austria, the Empress Maria Theresa. The war eventually became known as the War of Austrian Succession and lasted from 1740 to 1748. Prussia fought alongside several other states, including France, Bavaria and Saxony, which wished to join in the plunder of the Austrian Empire, whilst Maria Theresa had only Great Britain to assist her. Prussia emerged victorious, retaining the province of Silesia which Frederick had captured in the first weeks of the campaign.

The years of peace which followed (1748–56) were merely a truce. Maria Theresa was not reconciled to the loss of Silesia, and her diplomats worked to create a coalition of powers to punish Prussia for its previous aggression. The Seven Years War which resulted (1756–63) has a good as claim as any to be called an inevitable war. This time it was Prussia which found itself relatively isolated with only Great Britain as an ally. By contrast, Austria was supported by France and Russia. Despite the apparently overwhelming superiority of resources and manpower enjoyed by Austria and her allies, Frederick was able to hold onto Silesia and emerged in 1763 with his lands and prestige intact. The years after 1763 saw continued Austro-Prussian rivalry, and one more brief war, but after 1763 Maria Theresa accepted that Silesia was lost for ever.

These dramatic events, which dragged in the other powers of Europe and made Germany the focus of international affairs for half a century, have been the centre of much discussion by historians ever since. The debates have revolved around a number of important issues:

a) The Responsibility of Charles VI

To what extent was Austria's weakness in 1740 caused by Maria Theresa's father, the Emperor Charles VI (1711–40)? Could he, as the biographers of Maria Theresa claim, have done more to strengthen his state? To what extent did his foreign policy advertise Austrian weaknesses to others and encourage attack?

b) The Achievements of Frederick William I

Frederick William was responsible for strengthening the Prussian state and preparing it for war. To what extent should he therefore take the credit for Frederick II's victories?

c) The Causes of the Wars

To what extent were Frederick II's attacks in 1740 and 1756 unprovoked aggression? What were Frederick's long-term plans? Were the German historians of the nineteenth and twentieth centuries justified in claiming that Frederick aimed to take over the whole of Germany, or were his aims strictly limited to strengthening Prussia? Why did his attacks so quickly involve the rest of Europe in major wars? Would Frederick II have served Prussia better if, like his father, he had avoided wars?

d) The Prussian Victory

Why was Frederick II able to win his wars despite the heavy odds against him? How far was this due to Frederick's own skill and how far was it thanks to the work of his father and the mistakes of his enemies? What was the significance for Germany and for Europe of the Prussian victory? How did it effect European diplomacy after 1763? How did these wars affect other European states?

e) The Work of Maria Theresa

To what extent did Maria Theresa, through her domestic reforms, make up for her losses in the wars? Could she have done more to revive Austria? Was she a great ruler who held onto her Empire when many thought it was about to collapse, or was she an over-cautious and reactionary ruler who did little to strengthen her state?

f) The Work of Frederick II

How useful to Prussia were the lands Frederick conquered? How far did his wars weaken or strengthen the Prussian state? When he died in 1786, was Prussia stronger or weaker then when he inherited the throne in 1740? To what extent was Frederick responsible for the collapse of Prussia during the Napoleonic wars in 1806?

Before addressing the major issues of the causes and effects of Frederick's wars, you will need to have a clear understanding of the strengths and weaknesses of the two rival states, Prussia and Austria. It was these strengths and weaknesses which would ultimately decide the struggle for supremacy.

Making notes on 'Introduction: Habsburgs and Hohenzollerns'

It will be a good idea to familiarise yourself with the map of the Holy
Roman Empire. Whilst no examiner will expect you to know details of
eighteenth century borders, you will need to know the names of the
main states and provinces and where they lay in relation to each other.

You only need to make brief notes on this chapter. At this stage you
will want to be sure that you understand

- What the Holy Roman Empire was
- How it was governed
- The effects of seventeenth century wars on the Empire
- The supremacy of Austria.

When you have completed reading this book and making your notes,
you should feel confident about answering all the questions posed in
section 4 of the chapter. At this stage, you need only note the main
issues which you will be covering, so that you will keep these questions
in mind as you work through the book.

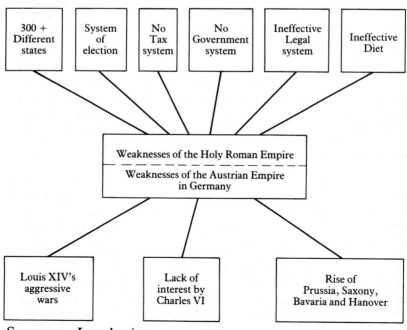

Summary – Introduction

CHAPTER 2

The Reign of Charles VI

1 The Strength of the State

Most eighteenth century European monarchs saw their highest priority as being the strengthening of their state. Although belief in the Divine Right of Kings – the idea that the monarch was chosen by God and must therefore always be obeyed – was no longer fashionable, this did not imply any reduction in the king's responsibilities or power. On the contrary, monarchs were expected to perform a wide variety of duties for the benefit of their state.

First and foremost, monarchs were expected to defend their people from conquest by other states. For many monarchs this was their primary aim, and this explains why most rulers spent such a large proportion of their taxes on the armed forces. Rulers were also expected to try to extend their own lands at the expense of others. It was assumed that conquests were always beneficial to a state, and that the price paid in terms of lives or money was one well worth paying. War was a natural and normal activity of a monarch, and military success and territorial conquest was the most important single factor in assessing a monarch's achievements in the eighteenth century. In domestic policy, the monarch was expected to provide a framework for society by issuing laws and ensuring through their enforcement that people had their rights respected and could carry on with their normal activities without fear of their neighbours. People had rights to be protected from crime to their person and to their own property, although the latter protection was very limited in the case of serfs. A state which was going to be able to support an effective army and to maintain law and order clearly required an efficient system of government, bureaucracy and taxation. Successful monarchs were those who were able to provide systems strong enough to survive the test of war.

It was becoming increasingly accepted that a major role of the monarch was both to protect and to stimulate the economy, and that this was not something that could be left entirely to the enterprise of the people. Under the fashionable theory of mercantalism, monarchs were expected to ensure a net inflow of gold into their territories. This was to be achieved by encouraging industry and exports whilst discouraging imports, usually through import duties, but sometimes through totally banning the bringing of certain categories of goods into the country. A healthy balance of trade would require other states to make up the difference with precious metals. A successful monarch was one who was able to protect his own economy from foreign competition, export as much as possible and import as little as possible. The gold thereby acquired within the state was a measure of its strength and could be used to finance wars.

In social matters, little was as yet expected from the monarch. Aspects of government activity which are regarded as important today – the provision of education, health care and the protection of people from starvation – were not seen as a major part of a monarch's role, although increasingly some rulers did accept that a basic provision of schools and protecting peasants from excessive demands from their nobles was in the state's interests. Such activities might lead to a better trained workforce, an improved economy, and the avoidance of civil wars.

One often underrated role of the monarch was his or her requirement to provide and train an heir. The strength of monarchy was its promise of continuing stable government. Nothing was feared more than the outbreak of a civil war – perhaps made worse by foreign intervention – because of a disputed succession. This was why the monarch was expected to have children and then to ensure that they were found suitable husbands or wives as quickly as possible. The price of a failure to ensure a smooth succession was well known. The Wars of Spanish, Polish and Austrian Succession were a powerful reminder to monarchs of the importance of providing an effective heir to the throne.

The successful monarch was one who was able to protect his people from foreign aggression, won wars and conquered land, provided law and order and a social framework which allowed the development of the economy, had an effective system of government and taxation, provided a minimum of educational and social provision, and who provided an adult trained heir to succeed him when he died. Some monarchs would add to this list the requirement to protect the state church and to persecute rival religions but this requirement, which had been a high priority for kings in previous centuries, was gradually declining in importance outside Austria and Spain. It was against this formidable list of expectations that Charles VI, Maria Theresa, Frederick William and Frederick II would be judged.

2 The Legacy of the Past

The Austrian Empire had an impressive pedigree. The first Habsburg prince had been elected Holy Roman Emperor as far back as 1273, and since 1438 every Emperor had come from this family. At the same time as they were establishing what looked like a hereditary right to the Imperial throne, the Habsburg princes had also been busy extending the domains of Austria. A combination of fortunate marriages, luck and (sometimes) skill had resulted in the Habsburgs emerging as one of the two great dynasties of Western Europe by 1500 – the other was the rulers of France. There was no question about Austria's status as a great power and, since the Habsburgs alone amongst European princes also carried the title of Emperor, they asserted the claim to be the pre-eminent family of Europe – or Catholic Europe at least.

The power and status of Austria had been called into question during the second half of the seventeenth century. The Thirty Years War (1618–48) had exhausted Austria as much as other German states, and in 1648 she had been forced to sign the humiliating Treaty of Westphalia which saw France replace Austria as the dominant state in Germany. It was therefore a difficult legacy which Leopold I (1658–1705) inherited. Leopold was an almost exact contemporary of Louis XIV of France, but was very different in his style of monarchy. Cold, serious and very religious, he was a most dutiful monarch, but one who found it difficult to make decisions. He put all his trust in God, and regarded both success and failure as God's judgements. Even the Pope's ambassadors found his calm assurance that God would decide the great matters of state surprising. A talented musician and composer, a man more at home in a church or a music room than on the battlefield or in a government office, Leopold was in many ways the worst person to rule a major power facing a crisis. Yet in the end he proved to be more successful than his rival, Louis XIV, who, enjoying far more power, a more centralised and efficient state, and having clear and aggressive aims, nevertheless ended his reign in defeat and bankruptcy whilst Austria was emerging from the wars in triumph. What were the reasons for this unexpected Austrian revival?

3 The Creation of the Danubian Empire

Leopold's foreign policy was dominated by two enemies. From the west he was threatened by France and from the east by a revived Ottoman Empire. Austria lacked the strength the fight both at once, so Leopold found himself having to make concessions to Louis XIV whilst he concentrated on the more immediate threat from the Turks. The Ottoman Empire declared war on Austria in 1682, and a large Turkish army laid siege to Vienna in 1683. Not for the last time, Austria was saved by external aid rather than by its own efforts. A multi-national army was formed to relieve Vienna – one of the rare occasions on which Christian states united against the common Muslim enemy. Significantly, France refused to contribute to the army. Although Louis XIV could not be seen actually to support Turkey in this contest, he had no intention of helping his major rival win a war; on the contrary, he had every expectation that he could use Austria's predicament to expand quietly into the Holy Roman Empire. The multi-national army drove off the Turks just as they were on the point of overrunning Vienna. The Turkish threat, which seemed so formidable in 1683, now collapsed in the face of defeat. Austrian armies, led by Prince Eugene of Savoy, won a series of victories against the Turks. In 1699, at the Treaty of

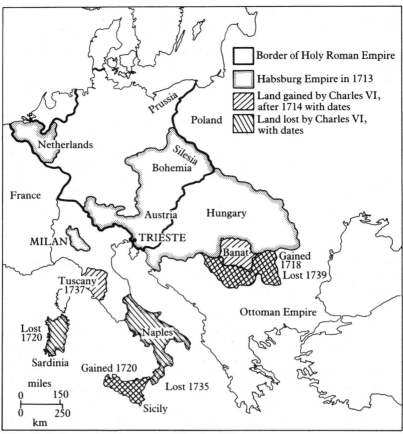

The Habsburg Empire under Charles VI

Karlowitz, the Turks lost all of Hungary, Transylvania, Croatia and Slovenia to the Austrians.

It had been a stunning and unexpected revival of Austrian fortunes. The Turkish threat had been eliminated, and Austrian land and power extended far to the south and east. The only disadvantages of these victories were that by her conquests Austria had become even less of a German state and more a multi-national state than before. Future Austrian rulers would find it difficult to reconcile the conflicting demands of different nationalities within the Empire whilst at the same time attempting to maintain leadership of the Holy Roman Empire and to create a unitary state.

With the Turkish threat ended, Leopold was at last able to turn his attention to the French. The Austrian army's performance in the War of Spanish Succession (1701–14) showed that whilst it might be competent enough to defeat the Turks, it was no match for the professional armies of Western Europe. When a Franco-Bavarian army invaded Germany in 1703, it seemed that once again the Austrian Empire was doomed. A serious revolt in Hungary (1703–11) added to the Emperor's problems. Even Austria's allies held out little hope for her survival. The Dutch ambassador to Vienna wrote home in 1703:

1 Everything here is quite desperate. The monarchy is on its last
legs and will collapse unless there is some divine intervention.
The enemy will soon be at the gates of Vienna. There is nothing
to stop them – no money, no troops, no defences. We will soon be
5 without bread. A general uprising is likely. You cannot imagine
with what unrestrained venom people speak of the Emperor,
government and clergy – yes, most bitterly of all the Jesuits who
will be the first victims of their rage.

Prince Eugene, in command of the Austrian army defending Vienna, not only agreed with this assessment, but came up with some forthright advice as to how to save the situation, advice which, as usual, Leopold rejected, preferring to trust in God:

1 The situation is graver than at any time in Habsburg history.
Extreme peril requires extreme measures. There are many wealthy families who have not made much sacrifice and should be
called upon to do so. Nor should the clergy be exempt. Our fight
5 is recognised the world over as a struggle for right and good. The
preservation of your subjects depends on the outcome, so everyone is bound to help. The state of the army is well known to Your
Majesty. Most of the soldiers have neither clothes nor money.
The officers are as poor as beggars. Many are dying, and when
10 they fall ill there is no-one to nurse them. None of the fortresses
have any reserves or supplies. There is not a magazine anywhere.
No one is paid. Nothing is heard but complaints.

Once again it was a multi-national army which saved Vienna. This time it was led by the Duke of Marlborough and it was victorious at the Battle of Blenheim (1704). Just twenty years after Turkey ceased to be a serious threat, the French threat was also removed.

Despite the relatively small part played by Austria in the War of Spanish Succession, she emerged with the largest territorial gains when peace was signed at Utrecht (1713) and Rastadt (1714), gaining the Netherlands, Milan, Naples and Sardinia from Spain. Austrian success at the peace conferences can be explained by the need to provide an effective counterweight to French power in Europe, and an increasing awareness that Austria was not powerful enough to be a threat to

European peace. Austria's large territorial gains were, in short, a recognition of Austria's *weakness* rather than her strength.

This war was immediately followed by a further war with Turkey (1716). Once again the indispensable Eugene was put in command of the Austrian armies, and once again he defeated the Turkish army in a series of battles. The Treaty of Passarowitz (1718) saw further gains for Austria, with the acquisition of the Banat and parts of Serbia and Wallachia (see the map on page 12).

Thus, in a relatively short space of time, Austria had emerged from decline to become an apparently large and powerful state. Yet these conquests, although impressive on paper, only increased the problems of managing a multi-national empire. These were problems which Leopold had hardly begun to address.

4 The Accession of Charles VI

When Leopold I died in 1705, he was succeeded by his eldest son, Joseph I. He only had a short reign, dying in 1711 aged 33 from smallpox, then frequently a fatal disease. As Joseph had no sons, the throne passed to his younger brother, who ascended as Charles VI. Charles was in theory King of Spain when the news that his elder brother had died reached him. He had been born in 1685 and had been put forward as the Habsburg claimant to the throne of Spain when it fell vacant in 1700. His candidature had been supported by Britain and Holland. When war broke out over the Spanish Succession, a British fleet had taken him to Spain, and there in 1704 he had been proclaimed king. Supported by the British navy, he had stayed in the country for about six years. However, most Spaniards had rallied to the rival Bourbon king, and it soon became clear that it was only British support which was keeping Charles in Spain at all. That support vanished in 1711 when Charles acceded to the Austrian throne. The British were as hostile to Spain being combined with Austria as they had been to its potential combination with France. Charles left Spain in 1711, never to return.

His years in Spain were to have a significant influence on the way Charles ruled Austria. It might have been expected that Spain would give Charles useful experience in ruling a state; in practice, his fascination with Spanish court ritual and his desire to re-establish power in Spain prevented him making any serious attempt to reform Austria.

5 Domestic Policy

By 1720 Austria was one of the largest states in Europe with a population (25 million) exceeded only by Russia and France. This superficial strength could not disguise serious underlying weaknesses in the Austrian system of government – weaknesses which neither Leopold I nor Joseph I had done anything to remedy.

a) The Court

One of the most important effects of Charles's stay in Spain was the effect it had on his style of government. Charles liked the formal court etiquette of Spain and introduced it into Austria. Court ceremonial became increasingly elaborate and obsequious. Nobody could now approach the Emperor without giving a deep bow. Even the highly structured and formal court etiquette of Louis XIV's Versailles could not compare with that of Charles VI.

It is difficult to assess the importance of this court ceremonial. It has been suggested that it significantly distanced the Emperor from his people and made it harder for his advisers to give him frank advice. This probably exaggerates its importance. Louis XIV had managed to combine formal court etiquette with effective government, so the two were not necessarily mutually exclusive.

Perhaps more significantly, the introduction of elaborate Spanish ritual was combined with lavish expenditure on the court. The royal palace, the *Hofburg*, was greatly extended, and he started the famous Spanish riding school in Vienna. These are features of Vienna which are much admired by tourists today and which are seen as an important part of Austria's heritage. The 2,000 paid court officials, to say nothing of the estimated 30,000 other hangers-on at the royal court, were also expensive. Nor was expense spared on furnishings or food for the royal family – or their pets. The royal parrots were washed in the most expensive wines rather than water! The contrast with Prussia's economical, not to say frugal, court life (see page 33) was obvious. Charles, it seems, was more interested in the appearance than the reality of power.

b) The Multi-national Empire

As early as 1526 Austria had ceased to be a purely German state when Bohemia and Moravia, with their Czech peoples, had been acquired. Since then every conquest had increased its non-German population and had given it ever-increasing territories outside the Holy Roman Empire. In 1720 the Austrian Emperor ruled not just Germans and Czechs, but also Hungarians, Rumanians, Serbs, Belgians, Italians and Slovenes. The German heartland was now a minor part of the state, both in area and as a percentage of the total population. This was in sharp contrast with most other states in Europe, where there had been a move towards the modern nation-state. The many different peoples of the Austrian Empire had nothing in common with each other and in some cases, such as the Netherlands and Naples, were geographically far removed from each other. The only common feature between them was that they happened to be ruled by the same monarch. In many parts of the Empire, Austrian officials were seen as foreigners, which was hardly surprising when the authorities sometimes practised persecution of the native population, as happened in Bohemia after 1618. Attempts to enforce royal control could lead to revolts against Austrian rule. The problem was particularly acute in Hungary, which had a long and proud tradition of independence, despite the fact that the kingdom had been nominally under either Ottoman or Austrian rule since 1526. There had been several major revolts against Habsburg rule, the most recent of which only crushed in 1711, the year in which Charles ascended the throne.

Of course, these problems were not of Charles's making. However, faced with the real problem of integrating a state with many different nationalities and languages, he took no action. On the contrary, he showed far greater respect than Leopold I had done for the different territories, maintaining the rights and privileges of local diets and nobles, and keeping royal control and interference to a minimum. It was not untypical that Eugene, his viceroy for the Netherlands, never felt it necessary to visit his province, leaving administration in the hands of local Belgian nobles. The result was that Charles never had to face revolts from discontented minorities as Leopold had done, and this may be counted as an achievement. Charles's easy-going rule over his nationalities earnt him a trouble-free reign in his Empire, but he had merely shelved a major problem. His failure to attempt any integration of his territories meant that a major weakness of the Empire remained. The experience of other states, including Prussia, suggests that welding together a divided state was a long-term process requiring in the first instance the establishment of an absolute monarchy as the key unifying force. Although it is highly unlikely that Charles could have achieved a full integration of his people during his lifetime, the fact remains that he did not even recognise the problem, let alone start the process of solving it.

c) The Multi-religious Empire

National rivalries were compounded by religious rivalries. The official religion of the state was Roman Catholicism, and Leopold had taken his responsibilities in this area very seriously. He had done this by giving full support to the Jesuit missionaries and by persecuting religious minorities. For the Protestants of Bohemia there had been the threat of arrest, torture and being sent as slaves to the galleys. Leopold had also crushed the growing Protestant movement in Austria itself. It is estimated that about 100,000 Protestants had gone into exile during his reign, so depriving the state of many of its most productive citizens. Jews had also been actively persecuted. However, none of these assertions of Catholic supremacy had prevented Leopold from seeking

Charles VI

and accepting subsidies in wartime from friendly Protestant states, such as Britain and the United Provinces (Holland).

Charles held the same strong beliefs. This was probably the result of a combination of the influence by his father and of his time in Spain. Although Jews were allowed back into Vienna, they were forced to live in a ghetto, wear distinctive yellow markings on their clothes, and pay special taxes. Protestants continued to be actively persecuted. By contrast, Charles was generous in his gifts to the Roman Catholic Church. Many new churches were built during his reign in the elaborate style known as baroque. Charles took his religious duties seriously, and those around him were obliged to follow suit. The French ambassador recorded:

> I have led a pious life here in Lent which has not left me free for a quarter of an hour. Only a monk could endure this life in Lent. I have spent altogether between Palm Sunday and Easter Wednesday, 100 hours with the Emperor in church.

The Austrian Catholic Church still retained wealth, power and privileges which churches in most other states had long since lost. The Church was exempt from taxation and owned considerable lands and wealth. It controlled nearly all education. Schools that existed offered a narrow theological education, usually taught in Latin. The church censored the press and books. New ideas were not encouraged. The result was intellectual sterility, as Wilhelm von Schroder, one of Leopold I's advisers, confirmed:

> They are so religious that they don't want to tinker with God's work. They want to keep things as it has pleased God to give them. Their great ignorance makes them sullen and negligent when it comes to work for themselves.

d) Central Government

The system of government (see the chart on page 19) looks at first glance to be a well-structured autocracy, with decisions flowing from the top. This impression is misleading. Central government was in fact extremely weak in Austria. The only organs of government which covered the entire Empire were the *Hofkammer*, which dealt with finances, the *Hofkriegrat*, covering war and the army, and the *Geheime Rat*, the Privy Council. These were committees of nobles, but they had only limited executive powers. There were no individual ministers or ministries in Austria. Joseph I had found the *Geheime Rat* too large and unwieldy, so had added a new tier, the *Geheime Konferenz* (Privy Conference), comprising 4 or 5 of his most trusted advisers. Yet even this group never developed into a cabinet, since the advisers did just that; they offered advice, but they made no decisions and had no power themselves.

Characteristic of the Austrian system of government were the separate chancelleries for each of the main areas of Austrian rule – Austria, Hungary, Transylvania, the Netherlands, and the Italian provinces. There was also a separate Chancellery for Imperial Affairs. These chancelleries were responsible for most areas of government business in each province. Instead of having, for example, a single department of justice for the whole Empire, there were different officials responsible for justice in each chancellery. This emphasised the disunity of the Empire. Inevitably the different chancelleries found themselves working against each other as they tried to develop their own provinces at the expense of others, rather than offering a state-wide system of government.

None of this might have mattered too much had the Habsburgs been effective and dynamic monarchs, able to work well with a team of able subordinates. It is clear from the structures that much depended on the personality and energy of the one person who held the whole Empire together. Unfortunately, both Leopold and Charles proved to be ineffective in this most crucial of all their responsibilities. Not only were they reluctant to take a lead in modernising the system of

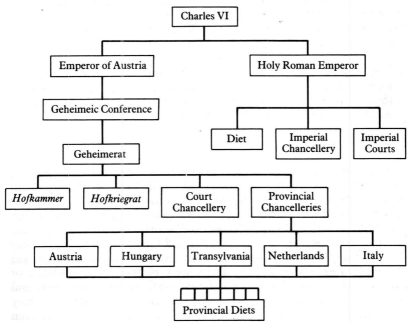

The System of Government in Austria under Charles VI

government, but they both chose poor ministers and then loyally supported them. The most notorious was Sinzendorf, who was at different times in charge of finance and foreign policy. He was a dilettante, inefficient and known to be corrupt, yet he held senior office throughout Charles's reign. When a capable person was given senior office, his advice was often ignored. Eugene, made responsible for running the Austrian army, bombarded Charles with suggestions for modernisation and reform. But nothing happened and Charles even expressed his pleasure when he heard that Eugene had died in 1735 – perhaps he was tired of being lectured.

It comes as no surprise to learn that Charles made no changes to the system of government inherited from his father and his brother. He was obliged to confirm the existing privileges and powers to the Diets in return for their approval of the Pragmatic Sanction (see pages 24–9). Charles was conscientious in the discharge of his duties, but had no wish to alter the existing system. He spent much of his time writing letters and instructions to his ministers and ambassadors, but this often led to long delays in making decisions, particularly during religious festivals or the hunting season. Although he seems to have gained the trust and liking of most of his advisers, he found it difficult to delegate work or to find advisers who could act on their own initiative. Even his ablest adviser, Bartenstein, a gifted and honest administrator, saw his role purely as carrying out orders and refused on principle ever to take decisions on his own.

e) Finances

The government was constantly short of money. The Habsburgs ruled a population two and a half times that of Britain, yet only received half the income. Most taxes were controlled by the provincial diets, which ensured that the state received the minimum of income. A few taxes were controlled from Vienna but these varied widely from one province to another – there was in fact not a single tax paid uniformly throughout the Empire – and were in any case often farmed out. Tax-farmers were made responsible for collecting a particular tax, and could keep a proportion of the proceeds for themselves. It was a recipe for corruption. Peasants were obliged to pay heavy taxes whilst the Tax-farmer only passed on a percentage to the government. This system also made it very difficult for the government to estimate how much money would come in during any year. What happened in 1736 was typical. In that year, when the state was in vital need of funds to support the two wars it was currently fighting, the total income from taxes was some 20 million guilders – less than half what had been expected. The result was an army constantly short of supplies, with the inevitable effect on its performance. The fact that Sinzendorf saw no need to make any alterations to the system did not help Austria's financial situation. The government relied increasingly on loans. By the end of Leopold's reign the state was already 60 million guilders in debt; during Charles's reign this increased to 100 million guilders. Borrowing money only solved the problem in the short term, and made the government dependant for its solvency on a handful of bankers. The death of Samuel Oppenheimer, who was handling the finances for the War of Spanish Succession, bankrupted the state overnight in 1703. Only generous subsidies from Britain and Holland enabled Austria to carry on with the war after that date. The Habsburgs' reliance on loans during the seventeenth and eighteenth centuries was a clear indication of its weakness.

f) The Economy   *in 1711...*

Charles was not unaware of Austrian economic backwardness, which was due to a large number of factors. These included the many internal customs barriers between different provinces, a shortage of labour (not helped, of course, by Charles encouraging thousands of Protestants to leave his lands), poor communications and the fact that the Austrian lands were sited in a part of Europe with no easy access to ports. The rigid enforcement of serfdom also helped prevent the mobility of labour which was needed for any large-scale economic development.

Charles was keen on developing overseas trade which he realised had been a major cause of the rise of British and Dutch power. Two commercial companies – the Ostend Company and the Fiume Company – were sponsored for this purpose by Charles but they enjoyed no lasting success. The former developed well until Charles was obliged to close it down after a few years as the price demanded by Great Britain and the United Provinces for their acceptance of the Pragmatic Sanction. The Fiume Company also failed – in this case because of lack of investment.

Charles did establish some industries financed by the government, including factories for candles, textiles and porcelain. However, such initiatives met with strong resistance from the guilds. These were another relic of medieval times, but they still exercised considerable power in Austria. They were groups of master craftsmen who controlled manufacturing in towns. Their resistance prevented Charles's new factories from developing into any threat to their monopoly. One important new road was built, linking Austria with the port of Trieste on the Adriatic coast (see the map on page 12). Unfortunately the development of Trieste as a major port was resisted by rivalry from Venice and the Maritime Powers (England and the United Provinces). In the end Charles was obliged to admit failure, abandoned his new Trading Companies and sold his merchant fleet to Venice. In contrast with this genuine if unsuccessful attempt to stimulate trade and industry, Charles did nothing to improve the conditions of the serfs or to encourage new developments in farming. Charles's economic policies

lack of overseas trade

were based on the Mercantalist ideas fashionable at the time. He had been rather unlucky in having to face such strong opposition to his plans from foreign states he dared not offend, but had also shown a notable reluctance to tackle those aspects of economic organisation within his state which he did have the power to deal with.

g) Local Government

The large Austrian provinces – such as Austria, Hungary and the Netherlands – were themselves divided into smaller provinces. Each of these small provinces had its own 'estates' or diet. This was an assembly made up largely of the local nobility. Typical was the diet of Lower Austria. This comprised 15 representatives of the Church, the Rector of Vienna University, 340 local nobles, and just one representative of the middle class of Vienna. The powers of these diets varied. The weakest were probably those of Bohemia, where most of the old Czech nobility had been deprived of their lands and titles after 1618 and replaced by Habsburg nominees. Amongst the most powerful were those in the Netherlands and Milan. These were former Spanish provinces used to running their own affairs. Very few Austrian officials were sent to these provinces. Such arrangements suited the local diets well. They continued to manage their own affairs, whilst being assured of Austrian protection against any possible French attack.

Most independent of all was the Hungarian diet. The nobles here even had their own separate coronation ceremony for their monarch, and they asserted a wide range of rights, including the right of rebellion, the right to choose their own monarch, and the right to veto any laws of which they did not approve. Leopold had at different times tried to reduce the rights of the Hungarian diet, but he had ultimately been obliged to recognise most of its powers. In return, most Hungarians accepted that they needed Austrian protection from Turkey. Ironically, the defeat of the Turks in 1699 may have encouraged the Hungarians to assert their rights again now that the Turkish threat had receded. The result was a serious Hungarian revolt (1703) which lasted eight years. Faced with such an assertive Hungarian nobility, there could be no question of Charles attempting to increase Austrian control over his most troublesome province, let alone asking the Hungarians to pay their fair share of taxes.

Each diet controlled most local taxes, deciding their scale, organising their collection, and deciding on how the income would be spent. They were often responsible for recruiting and maintaining a quota of soldiers. The result was a patchwork of different systems of government. It is true that Austria did have officials in each province, but since these were usually the same nobles who were active in the diet, local interests still remained paramount.

During the reigns of Leopold and Charles, the diets of Austria and Hungary did become less active. This was mainly because many of the richest nobles moved into Vienna where they built fine houses and became part of the Austrian court. They were therefore much less involved in the affairs of their local diet. It is possible that both monarchs actively encouraged nobles to come to Vienna – in the same way as Louis XIV had invited the powerful French nobles to enjoy themselves at Versailles – in order to reduce their power. It is more likely, however, that this was an incidental effect of the expansion of court life under the two emperors.

The diets played a major role in both resisting any tendency towards absolute rule, and in increasing social divisions. In many provinces the diets ensured that nobles paid no taxes. In some of the provinces, including Milan, Hungary and the Netherlands, royal power was so weak that the nominal Governor-General rarely bothered to visit his province. The diets in Bohemia and Hungary were active in enforcing and increasing the burdens of serfdom on the peasants, and also took the lead in persecuting non-Catholics. The continued survival of the diets was therefore a major cause of Austrian disunity, weakness and the survival of noble power. The contrast with Prussia, where the king had established a strong centralised government and reduced the diets to impotence, is revealing.

h) Conclusion

Austria under Charles VI was an extremely limited monarchy. He had neither the power nor the inclination to reform his disunited empire. The long and vulnerable borders of his state were protected by an army of barely 80,000 men – less than half the size of the French army. Despite all of Eugene's pleas, no attempt was made to increase the size of the army, or to modernise the system of training. There was no systematic conscription as there was in Prussia. Instead, the army relied on provincial quotas, which were usually met by use of the press-gang. Senior officers were always nobles, who often had no military experience at all, having bought their posts. Junior officers were badly paid and, unless they had their own sources of income, found it almost impossible to gain promotion.

Charles was in charge of a system of government which actually encouraged the disunity inherent in his empire, and he also had one of the weakest financial systems of any state in Europe. Although some advisers, notably Eugene, urged Charles to make reforms, the emperor's complacency was about the state of his realm was shared by most of his ministers. The old Austrian state did not fail until after Charles died, but he must bear some responsibility for the collapse of 1740–2.

6 The Problem of the Succession

Charles VI was to enjoy a long reign as Emperor of Austria, from 1711 to 1740. Yet almost as soon as he became Emperor he was anxious about what would happen if he died without having a son. To prepare for this eventuality, he produced a document in 1713 which has become known as the Pragmatic Sanction. At the time his worries must have seemed fantastic. He was then only 28 years old and married to the 16 year old Elizabeth Christina. There was no reason to think they should not have sons. However, Charles's concerns at this early date were not as unreasonable as some historians have suggested. There are a number of reasons for this.

Most immediately frightening for Charles was the fact that his older brother Joseph had been fairly young and in good health when he had died suddenly from smallpox without having a son. Charles was very conscious that the same fate could befall him. He was also very aware that if he died without a son to survive him there would be no male Habsburg to inherit the throne. His own recent experience in Spain told him what would probably happen next. When Carlos 'the bewitched' of Spain had died without a male heir in 1700 the result had been a long war as rival claimants fought over the inheritance. There was every reason to suppose that the same would happen in Austria if he were to die without a son. There were three possible male claimants to the Austrian throne from abroad (see the family tree on page 25). Charles, Duke of Bavaria, and Augustus, Elector of Saxony, were married to the two daughters of Joseph I, whilst none other than Philip V, Charles's old rival as King of Spain, could also claim the throne through a very distant relationship with the Habsburgs going back four generations.

Charles's wife did give birth to a son in 1716, but he died after a few months. His daughter, Maria Theresa, was born in 1717, and she was soon followed by another girl. However, the longed for son never appeared. By 1725 it was clear that Elizabeth Christina, although still a relatively young woman, was not going to have any more children. The hypothetical problem of the succession had become real.

The fact that Charles's heir was female only added to his problems. To the threat of foreign intervention was added the distinct possibility that the Empire would break up internally. There had never been a female ruler in Austria, and it was possible that some provinces might invoke the ancient Salic Law, which prevented inheritance through the female line, and find alternative rulers. Hungary in particular was only obliged to accept a Habsburg ruler so long as he was male. Should the male line die out, the Hungarian diet was empowered to elect its own monarch.

* In short, Charles was justified in his concerns about the succession, and right to give the problem high priority. Whether he was right in the

*See Preface for explanation of * symbol

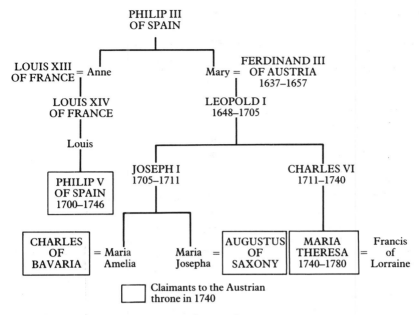

The Claimants to the Austrian Succession

methods he used is another matter. The Pragmatic Sanction, first issued in 1713 and later revised, was his method of solving the problem. It stated that in the event of Charles not having a son, the throne should pass to his eldest daughter, rather than to any other claimant.

* Charles made his document public in 1719 and started his lifetime's work – to have the Pragmatic Sanction approved by all those who could influence events, both inside and outside the Habsburg Empire. He wanted the reassurance before he died that both his provincial diets and the powers of Europe were willing to accept his daughter as the rightful ruler of Austria. There could be no question of Maria Theresa becoming Holy Roman Emperor – the Salic Law undoubtedly applied to the Empire – but he did hope that the Electors would accept Maria Theresa's eventual husband instead.

The first stage was to persuade the various provincial diets to accept the Pragmatic Sanction. This proved to be relatively easy. By 1722 they had all accepted the document in return for Charles agreeing to maintain their priveliges and powers. At this stage, therefore, Charles could be well pleased with his achievement. He had ensured that his empire would not fall apart when he died and, indeed, all the diets honoured their undertakings and accepted Maria Theresa as their ruler in 1740.

* It is when we turn to Charles's attempts to gain acceptance of the

Pragmatic Sanction by the rest of Europe that the extent of his achievement is more in doubt. It was not as if he was short of advice. Prince Eugene, his most experienced general and by now the Empire's elder statesman, put it succintly. What was needed, Eugene said, was not paper promises but a large army and a full treasury. That would be a far greater deterrent to potential aggressors than a document. Charles rejected the advice. He felt strongly about the value of diplomacy and he considered himself to be a skilful negotiator. It is likely that the ease with which he persuaded his own diets to accept the document encouraged him to use the same method abroad.

One by one the powerful states of Europe agreed to accept the Pragmatic Sanction. Charles was so anxious to gain the acceptance of the European states that he was willing to make substantial political or economic concessions in return for a signature. Bavaria and Saxony, ruled by the two most likely rival claimants for the Austrian throne, accepted as early as 1720. Other states followed, until even Austria's old enemy France accepted the document in 1738. On the surface, the whole affair of the Pragmatic Sanction had been a total success. After twenty-five years of hard work every provincial diet and European power had accepted it. Charles was confident that, when he died, Maria Theresa would ascend the throne without serious opposition.

* The reality was quite different. By hawking around the document, Charles had in fact been exposing Austrian weakness and reminding Europe of the weakness of his daughter's claim. Had he combined this policy with Eugene's advice, it would not have mattered, but he had used the Pragmatic Sanction as a substitute for any real strengthening of the state. His simple faith that rulers would keep their promises was not dissimilar to his father's. Such faith, whilst admirable in an ordinary citizen, was unrealistic in the hard world of eighteenth century politics.

7 Foreign Policy

In his first few years as Emperor, Charles was able to reap the benefits of Leopold's successful wars against France and the Ottoman Empire. The peace treaties of Rastadt (1714) with France and Passarowitz (1718) with the Ottoman Empire saw substantial gains for Austria. These, combined with the evident decline of France, the Ottoman Empire, Spain and the United Provinces, meant that Austria was now potentially the strongest state in Europe.

Charles followed an active foreign policy. He was a strong believer in the importance of diplomacy and established a series of alliances, most of them short-lived. He intrigued unsuccessfully in Spain and Italy, but after 1725, as the Pragmatic Sanction came to dominate his reign, his foreign policy was dictated by the need to make concessions to other powers in return for their support of the precious document. It was also the Pragmatic Sanction which forced him to undertake two wars which were to seriously weaken Austria in the 1730s.

One of the most important people to sign the document was Augustus of Saxony, since his was one of the strongest claims to the Austrian throne, should Maria Theresa not be acceptable. Augustus's acceptance had only been obtained on condition that Austria supported his claim to the Polish throne when it fell vacant. Poland was at that time ruled by Augustus's father, Augustus II, but, like the Holy Roman Empire, its throne was elective, not hereditary. When Augustus II died, Charles dutifully supported Augustus III's claim to succeed him, as did Russia. Unfortunately there was a rival candidate, Stanislas Lesczinski, who was supported by Louis XV of France. The result was the War of Polish Succession (1733–8) between Augustus, supported by Austria and Russia, and Stanislas, supported by France. The Austrian army did not perform well in this war, and at the Treaty of Vienna lost a substantial portion of its lands in Italy, but at least Charles had the satisfaction of obtaining French support for the Pragmatic Sanction.

* At the same time a much greater humiliation was taking place. This was also a result of promises made in return for acceptance of the Pragmatic Sanction. Austria had agreed to join Russia in a war with the Ottoman Empire as a condition of obtaining Empress Anna's approval of the Pragmatic Sanction. Fighting between Russia and the Ottomans broke out in 1736. Charles felt obliged to support the Russians; victory here might provide compensation for the lost land in Italy. The war was a disaster. When the Turks won the major battle of Crocyka in 1739, it became clear that the war was lost. Austrian humiliation was complete when peace was made at Belgrade in 1739. Austria was forced to cede to the Ottoman Empire most of the land she had conquered in the previous war (see the map on page 12).

* The balance sheet on Charles's foreign policy undoubtedly shows more losses than gains. Charles had spent 29 years playing the game of diplomacy with very little effect. He had lost lands, virtually bankrupted his state through his wars, and lost all the prestige so carefully (and artificially) built up by Leopold. Neither his efforts to win acceptance for the Pragmatic Sanction, nor his ambitious diplomatic manoeuvres had ultimately been of much benefit to Austria. Above all, the defeats suffered by the Austrian army between 1734 and 1739 showed other European leaders that the Austrian army was not be feared.

One man who took particular note of Austrian weakness was Frederick, the heir to the Prussian throne. As early as 1739 he had decided that Austria was vulnerable to attack. Charles had now advertised Austrian weakness both through the Pragmatic Sanction and through his defeats in war. It was not, perhaps, the best of inheritances to leave his daughter.

8 Assessment

a) The Death of Charles VI

In 1740 Charles was aged 55 and had enjoyed good health. However, the defeats in the recent wars had broken him. He claimed that they had taken ten years off his life. Nevertheless, his death in October 1740 was as sudden and unexpected as that of his elder brother in 1711. He probably died from food-poisoning after accidentally eating some poisonous mushrooms – the dish of mushrooms, as Voltaire observed, which changed the history of Europe. The event for which he had planned for so long had finally come about. Rarely in history has a ruler spent so long preparing for what would happen after he died. And rarely in history have so many elaborate precautions been to so little avail.

b) Conclusion

There can be little doubt that Charles's reign was unsuccessful. When he died, the state was in debt to the tune of 100 million guilders, whilst the treasury held only 70,000 guilders. The army was made up of only 80,000 men who were poorly equipped, poorly trained and suffering from low morale after their recent defeats.

To what extent should Charles take the blame for these failures? Historians have varied in their judgements, but on the whole he has been sharply criticised, particularly when compared to his daughter. Several of Maria Theresa's biographers have stressed Charles's failures, if only to emphasise how well Maria Theresa did under the circumstances. Why did he not heed the advice of Eugene? Why did he put his trust in pieces of paper? He could and should have made major reforms of his army, government and finances. Why did he not follow the examples of Walpole in England, Fleury in France and Frederick William in Prussia by putting top priority on domestic affairs and avoiding foreign entanglements as far as possible?

* One of the few historians to defend Charles has been Penfield Roberts. In his book *The Quest for Security*, he argued that it is much too simple to say Charles should and could have made reforms. Austria was a complex multi-national state and it was not possible to turn it into a unitary state such as France or Prussia. Too much of its territory had only recently been acquired and could not be turned overnight into a tightly integrated empire. Charles was, in fact, in tune with the aspirations of both his subjects and his advisers. Roberts also argued that Eugene's constant demands for military reforms should not be taken too seriously. He was himself the commander of the army for many years, and proved to be as dilatory about making reforms when he had the chance to do so as he was in governing his province of the

Netherlands. In short, Eugene was too quick to blame Charles for his own failures. Finally, the Pragmatic Sanction was not a waste of time. Without it, the provinces might have broken away in 1740, and for all its faults it gave Maria Theresa a powerful weapon after 1740. It gave her a legal right to the throne and the moral authority to rule which might otherwise have been lacking.

Roberts's analysis is a useful corrective to the usual dismissal of Charles as an incompetent ruler with a taste for useless pieces of paper and well-washed parrots. However, it does, perhaps, go too far towards the other extreme, for Roberts ignores Charles's religious persecutions and his failure to take any real steps to encourage the economy. There were many aspects of Austrian government which were capable of being reformed, even if the multi-national nature of his empire could not be waved away. By any standards he was naive to think that international approval of the Pragmatic Sanction was worth anything. Indeed, even by his own standards he had no reason to feel complacent about the international scene. For one thing, despite all Austria's pressure, the Elector of Bavaria insisted on maintaining his claim to the Austrian throne. Bavaria was only a small state and in no position to enforce the claim on its own. Unfortunately there were worrying indications that, despite acceding to the Pragmatic Sanction, France might yet support the Bavarian claim, since Fleury refused to renounce his earlier support for the Bavarians even after 1738. France, in short, could still choose which candidate to back when the time came.

A balanced assessment might give Charles some credit for his early awareness of the problem of the succession, and obtaining the support of the diets for the Pragmatic Sanction. Whilst Roberts may well be right to say that there was only a limited amount Charles could have done to reform and modernise his state, it remains true that the King did not even try to do the things that were possible. In the final analysis it remains surprising that a ruler so conscious of the need to prepare for the future, did so little of practical use for his daughter.

Making notes on 'The Reign of Charles VI'

Whilst making your notes, you will need to bear in mind the key questions concerning the reign of Charles VI.
i)   What were the weaknesses of the Austrian Empire in 1711?
ii)   To what extent (if any) had these weaknesses been overcome by 1740?
iii) To what extent should Charles VI be held personally responsible for these weaknesses?
This chapter includes a number of charts, maps and date lists. You

need not worry too much about them. They are reference diagrams to enable you to understand the complexities of eighteenth century Austria. You would not be expected to reproduce the details in the examination. In short, it is important that you understand the *significance* of what is in the diagrams, rather than their details.

Source based questions on 'The Reign of Charles VI'

1 The Crisis of 1703
Study the extracts from the Dutch ambassador's report, and from Prince Eugene on page 13. Then answer the following questions:
a) Who, according to these sources, was being blamed for the crisis? *(4 marks)*
b) What solutions does Eugene suggest for the crisis? *(4 marks)*
c) One source was written by the ambassador of a country allied with Austria; the other by Austria's senior general. From the authorship and contents of these sources, discuss how useful these sources are to a historian assessing how serious the crisis of 1703 was. *(6 marks)*
d) 'These sources were written in 1703, but they could just as easily have been written in 1739'. Discuss what this remark means, and how true it is. *(6 marks)*

2 The importance of religion
Study the extracts on page 18, and then answer the following questions:
a) The French ambassador was himself a Catholic. Why, then, does he object to spending time in church with the Emperor? *(4 marks)*
b) What does this extract suggest about Charles VI's priorities? *(4 marks)*
c) What does von Schroder suggest are the effects of the power of the church on Austria? *(6 marks)*
d) Using both these extracts and your own knowledge, discuss the view that the power of the Roman Catholic church was one of the main causes of the weakness of Austria during the reign of Charles VI. *(6 marks)*

CHAPTER 3

Frederick William I

1 The Early Years

Prussia in 1713 was no longer a state which could easily be ignored by the rest of Europe. Previous rulers had increased its territory and prestige. A start had been made in centralising the government and in reducing the privileges of the nobles. However, Prussia was still far from being a great power. Her lands were too scattered and difficult to defend, the economy was still undeveloped, the population was low, and the government was still dependent on subsidies from more powerful states in Europe. Frederick I's creation of a monarchy had been expensive, and the government faced bankruptcy. It was a mixed inheritance for the new king, Frederick William, when he ascended the throne in 1713.

Frederick William I had been born in 1688, the year in which his father had became Elector of Brandenburg. Like his father, Frederick William was a pious man, deeply affected by his Lutheran upbringing. However, in other respects he had little in common with Frederick I. Frederick William was not merely uninterested in music, the arts and the sciences: he despised them. Instead, he took an early interest in military matters. Already as a young boy, he saved his pocket money to buy uniforms for the small troop of cadets of his own age that he drilled. When he was sent to take part in the War of Spanish Succession he struck up a life-long friendship with Prince Leopold of Anhalt-Dessau, a tough warhorse who left the running of his tiny principality to his wife whilst he indulged his love of war. Prince Leopold was to become one of the formative influences both on Frederick William personally and on the Prussian army.

On his return to Berlin, Frederick William was appalled at the corruption and mismanagement of the finances he found at his father's court. It was Frederick William who carefully established the extent of the corruption and presented the damning evidence to his father in 1711. Frederick I had no choice but to sack the apparently all-powerful Prime Minister, Wartenburg. With his fall, Frederick William took over the effective management of the state. Although court life would be allowed to continue as long as his father lived, few courtiers could have had any illusions about their chances of survival once Frederick William became king. There were also other indications that Frederick William would prove to be very different from his father. As Crown Prince, he was notoriously mean, to the point of being miserly. He was already suffering from recurring bouts of ill-health. He was insensitive, bad-tempered, violent and subject to rapid changes of mood. He had a cruel sense of humour, which was typified by an incident when he and

Frederick William I

Prince Leopold cut off the tails of all the cows in a field as a little joke on the farmer. He openly despised people and things not from his narrow world – particularly intellectuals, bureaucrats, foreigners, Jews, Jesuits, scientists, musicians and anything from France. His only apparent pleasures were hunting, over-eating, drinking, smoking and sharing coarse practical jokes with soldiers. He had an interest in tall soldiers – already as Crown Prince all the men in his bodyguard were over six feet tall. Yet he combined these crude and violent traits with high moral standards and a strong sense of duty. He was completely faithful to his wife in an age of lax morality among royalty. He denounced prostitution and said there were no such things as mistresses, only harlots and whores. This strange mixture of duty and cruelty, high morals and boorish anti-intellectualism, would seem to make Frederick William an unlikely candidate to be the founder of modern Prussia.

When Frederick I died in 1713 his son gave him a magnificent and expensive funeral. It was a last act of respect to his dead father. Formalities over, Frederick William got down to business. After symbolically throwing away the wig he had been obliged to wear, he asked to see the list of servants at court. Two thirds of them were sacked at once, and the rest suffered dramatic cuts in their salaries and privileges. The average pay cuts were around 75 per cent, with a few unlucky ones suffering a 90 per cent reduction. The jewels, wines, coaches, fine furniture and zoo animals were all sold. His Master of Ceremonies found that he no longer had any work to do and moved to Saxony where his talents were in greater demand. The members of Frederick's famous orchestra and all his singers were dismissed. The court architect was given no further work and moved to Russia. Frederick William sold all but five of the twenty-five palaces and houses his father had owned. Even this figure is misleading, because all five were turned into government offices and the gardens into parade grounds for his soldiers. Frederick William, his wife and children (he had 14 in all, but most failed to survive for more than a few months) lived in just five rooms in a corner of one of the palaces. The King of Prussia now lived more modestly than most of the middle-class merchants of Berlin. The savage cuts extended to servants of the royal family. His mother was allocated just two servants, whilst he was so mean with his own servants that his wife and daughters had to do the cleaning and sweeping themselves. The royal stables were cut from 1,000 to 30 horses. When he was crowned king at Konigsberg, the whole ceremony cost just 2,500 thalers, compared to the five million thalers that his father had spent on his coronation. Royal meals were now modest bourgeois affairs, with the family helping themselves to meat, cheese and beer. Frederick William even checked the kitchen accounts himself. It was said that he complained if a few more eggs were used than he had allowed for. It was all a far cry from the extravagence of Frederick I's court. It also revealed a totally different attitude towards the role of the monarch to that of his contemporary, Charles VI of Austria, with his 30,000 courtiers.

Frederick William's meanness over court expenditure had two important effects. First, there was a dramatic saving of money. Under Frederick I court expenditure had averaged 400,000 thalers a year, or 12–13 per cent of the total state budget. His son spent only 1 per cent of the budget on the court, and resented every thaler of that. The money saved meant that more could be spent on the army. The other effect was to help turn Prussia into an object of ridicule throughout Europe. How could one take seriously a king who made his wife do the washing-up? How could one respect a monarch who added up how much milk his

servants drank every week? The overall effect was that foreign states-
men tended to overlook the crucial changes that were taking place
inside Prussia.

2 Frederick William's Philosophy

Frederick William's political philosophy was simple. Prussia was a
weak and divided state that could be turned into a strong and united
country. The way to achieve this was through sound finances and a
large, well-equipped army. A system of absolute monarchy in which all
would obey the monarch unquestioningly was the way to create unity.
He also insisted that everyone had an obligation to serve the state, and
to work hard and honestly for it. This rule applied most of all to
himself. Not for him the idea that as king he could enjoy himself; on the
contrary, he was there to set an example to others. None of this came
from writers or from published theories – both of which were among
the long list of things Frederick William distrusted. They came partly
from his personal experience of seeing what damage extravagence and
corruption had done to his father's realm, and partly from the teachings
of the Bible.

Frederick William's beliefs were often expressed in simple and
absolute statements. The following examples give a flavour of his
philosophy:

1 Tell the Prince of Anhalt that I am the finance minister and the
  field marshal of the King of Prussia. This will uphold the King of
  Prussia as he should be upheld.
  God placed me on the throne, not to be idle, but to work, and rule
5 his land well.
  I am master and king and must be obeyed.
  The soul is God's. Everything else is mine.
  One must serve the king with life and limb, with goods and
  chattels, with honour and conscience, and surrender everything
10 except salvation. The latter is reserved for God. But everything
  else must be mine.
  I pay them [civil servants] to work.

Frederick William felt that, armed with these simple truths, he could
not go far wrong. The first step was to reform the army.

3 The Army

a) Military Reforms

Frederick William was obsessed by the army. He expressed his views
on the necessity of a large army in a letter to his son in 1725.

1 Fritz, think about what I tell you. Always maintain a good and
large army. You can have no better friend and you cannot
maintain yourself without one. Our neighbours want nothing
better than to overthrow us. I know their aims, and you will get to
5 know them as well. Pay no attention to vanities, but stick to
reality. Always think highly of a good army and money, out of
which the glory and security of a prince is made.

The new monarch started his reign by disbanding some of the colourful
bodyguards with whom his father liked to surround himself. He then
set about expanding his forces with real soldiers. His close friend Prince
Leopold of Anhalt-Dessau was put in command of the army, and was
responsible for many of the reforms now introduced. Prince Leopold
brought about important changes in the way the soldiers fought. He
replaced the wooden ramrod with one made of iron. This apparently
trivial change was in fact very important. Wooden ramrods were likely
to break during a battle. The iron ramrod was both more reliable and
enabled faster loading of muskets. This change, combined with
improved training, enabled Prussian soldiers to fire their muskets six
times a minute. Other armies could barely manage two rounds a
minute. This formidable increase in firepower alone turned the Prussian army into the most efficient in Europe. At the same time he made a
change to the way bayonets were fixed to muskets. Now it was
permanently attached to the outside, so that Prussian soldiers could fire
and then charge with the bayonet at once. Other armies had to fix
bayonets after firing. This again gave Prussian soldiers a significant
advantage in time when charging (or resisting a charge) after firing their
muskets.
   Prince Leopold went on to introduce something we take for granted
in armies today; marching in formation. Training soldiers to march in
unison was harder than allowing them to walk at their own pace as other
armies did. However, it had huge advantages. It enabled them to move
faster than other armies, which had to wait for the stragglers. In an age
when the infantry walked to the battlefield, a slight advantage in speed
was critical. Marching together enabled them to attack and fire
simultaneously. Finally there were the intangible benefits. The tramp
of many boots marching together sounded both sinister to the waiting
enemy, and encouraged *ésprit de corps* amongst the men.
   Both Frederick William and Leopold recognised the need for a
well-trained army. They relentlessly drilled and trained their men
personally. The army was re-equipped with the latest muskets and
artillery. Fortresses were built and manned, and magazines of guns and
gunpowder were established. Powder and textile factories were built
under state patronage to supply the ammunition and the plain blue
uniforms which replaced the gaudy but impractical uniforms of
Frederick I's army. Frederick William believed in harsh discipline. He

believed that soldiers only fought effectively if they were more afraid of their own officers than of the enemy. Floggings and executions were the punishments for misbehaviour, and the Prussian army enjoyed the doubtful honour of being the most brutal in Europe. This harsh discipline did not stop (and may have encouraged) widespread desertions amongst his men, averaging 1,000 a year. Frederick William thought this was a small price to pay for the creation of soldiers who would unhesitatingly obey orders.

Frederick William inherited an army of reasonable size considering the extent of his territory. However, the 40,000 men were not enough for the purposes he envisaged. During his reign the army was steadily expanded until it reached the astonishing strength of 83,000 men in 1740. This gave Prussia the fourth largest army in Europe – only those of Russia, France and Austria were larger. Yet Prussia was only the tenth largest European state in area and the twelfth largest in population. No other state had such a high proportion of its men in uniform. In France, which had the largest population and the largest army at this time, 1 person in 150 was a soldier. In Prussia it was 1 person in 25. As a proportion of adult males it was 1 in 5. How did Frederick William manage to impose this apparently impossible burden on his people?

Not all the soldiers who fought under the Prussian flag were in fact native Prussians. The proportion of foreigners in the army varied from time to time, and different historians offer different estimates. But a reasonable, if rough, general estimate would seem to be that about half the Prussian army was made up of foreign mercenaries. Prussia (along with most other European states) had always used mercenaries. Relying too heavily on mercenaries was risky, as Frederick William recognised. On the one hand they were professional soldiers and relieved the burden of conscription on his own people. On the other hand, they were expensive to hire and, since they fought for money not patriotism, they did not always fight with as much determination as native troops. However, Frederick William knew he could not manage without them if he wished to expand the army.

Even with the help of foreign mercenaries, there were much increased demands on Prussian men to fill the swelling ranks of the army. In 1733 Frederick William found the solution to his recruitment problem with the introduction of the canton system. Prussia was divided into districts called cantons. Each canton was required to supply a quota of troops each year. Local officials took lists of possible young men when they reached the age of 12. The appropriate number of boys were then taken from the lists each year and were conscripted into the army for 20 years. The lists only applied to peasants. In line with common European practice at this time, nobles were exempt from conscription. Unusually, the middle classes and industrial workers were also exempt. The system was not as onerous and arbitrary as it appeared on the surface. Frederick William was well aware that the young men were needed back on their farms, and that by recruiting too many peasants he was in danger of irretrievably impoverishing his state. So after two years or so rigorous training in a local town within the canton, the soldier was allowed to return home. He was still required to attend retraining and manoeuvres for between two and three months each year during peacetime thereafter, but otherwise was free to work as a civilian.

This system had several advantages. It was much less onerous on the peasants. Being conscripted only involved two years full-time service, rather than the 25-year nightmare endured by peasants in Russia. Even during these first two years, the recruit lived near enough to home to see his family from time to time. Releasing soldiers for at least nine months of each year afterwards greatly reduced the costs to the state. It meant that at any one time only about a quarter of the native soldiers were actually being drilled, trained and fed. The peasant could continue to contribute to the economy, but was available at once as a trained reservist should war break out.

The system was so efficient and cheap that one is led to question why other countries did not copy it. Other states did indeed organise armed forces locally, but these were poorly trained militia of little military value and were quite separate from the army. The Prussian system worked, partly because the small size of the state enabled the scattered groups of soldiers to be rapidly concentrated if necessary, and because the training was so rigorous. It was only after the Prussian army demonstrated its efficiency during the reign of Frederick II that other states started to adopt its principles. Prussia had invented the nation-in-arms. The army was not merely strengthening the state. In many ways the Prussian army *was* the state.

b) The Nobles and the Army

At the same time as organising an efficient recruitment system for peasants, Frederick William was also integrating the *Junkers* into the army. The king was well aware of the continuing privileges and power enjoyed by the nobility, and that they represented a major obstacle to his plans to unify his state under royal control. His solution was to reserve posts in the officer corps for nobles. Lists were made of young male nobles when they reached the age of 12. Frederick William personally selected those who were to attend his newly founded cadet school for the training of officers. From then on promotion was by merit. It was a system of conscription or state service not dissimilar to that used for the peasants. Noble resentment at this enforced service was overcome in various ways. Officers were paid well, and the income was useful to the nobles, many of whom were finding that the wealth generated by their serfs was no longer sufficient to maintain their standard of living. More important was the high social status accorded to officers. Frederick William set the example by always wearing military uniform (a habit later copied by royalty in other states). He drastically altered the Table of Ranks, the official list giving orders of precedence. The number of ranks was slashed from 142 to 46 and in the process civilian ranks were demoted, whilst army officers were promoted. A general, for instance, went up from 19th to 9th position in the table, and the top rank was held by a field-marshal, who was now rated as being more important than a minister. Frederick William surrounded himself with army officers, from whom he selected his only friends. His two closest advisers, Leopold and Grumbkow, were both field-marshals. He made no secret of his preference for army officers – 'I would rather have 50,000 soldiers than 100,000 ministers'. He demanded high standards from his officers, and sacked those who proved unreliable. Strict rules were laid down about behaviour and honesty. Officers were forbidden, for instance, to have mistresses. Gradually the *Junkers* came to welcome appointment in the army, which offered companionship, high social status, close links with the king, and an opportunity to win fame and honour. A strong *ésprit de corps* developed among the *Junker* officers. The domination of the Prussian officer corps by the *Junkers* would put a unique stamp on the army. They retained their undue influence even after the Hohenzollerns were deposed, and it was not finally removed until 1945.

c) How Effective were Frederick William's Reforms of the Army?

Historians have identified only two real weaknesses in the Prussian army. One was the quality of the cavalry, which was less well-trained than the infantry or artillery and was to perform disappointingly in Frederick II's wars, and the other was Frederick William's obsession with very tall soldiers. He formed a regiment of these giants, known as the Potsdam Grenadiers or simply 'The Blue Boys'. Eventually the regiment numbered about 3,000 men. He drilled this group endlessly and knew many of the men by name. In this regiment it was a matter of the taller the better. None were shorter than six feet, and the tallest were nine feet tall. When their hats were added, they reached up to ten feet. Frederick William, himself only a modest five feet three inches tall, spent a fortune on his regiment. Not only in Prussia, but all over Europe, his agents went searching for giants. Those that could not be bought – and he was willing to pay up to 6,000 thalers for a good specimen – were kidnapped. Many stories were told about the extreme lengths to which the king would go in order to obtain tall soldiers. He even tried (unsuccessfully) to breed a new generation of giants by ensuring that his Grenadiers only married exceptionally tall women. Other monarchs were quick to spot his weakness for tall men, and sent giants to him as presents. He freely admitted he would do anything to get tall soldiers: 'He who sends me tall soldiers can do with me whatever he likes', he said on one occasion, and on another, 'the most beautiful girl would be a matter of indifference to me. But tall soldiers! They are my weakness!'. He had life-size portraits painted of some of his favourites and would bore foreign guests by taking them to see the collection and talking about his men. When he was ill – which was much of the time – nothing cheered him up more than having some of his tallest men march round and round his bedroom.

A psychologist might enjoy finding plausible explanations for Frederick William's obsession with giants who, needless to say, were much too precious in his eyes to ever be sent into battle. For the historian the problem is simpler. What *effect* did these giants have and was the king aware of the effects? The rest of Europe laughed at Frederick William's foible. It seemed to prove that the man was harmless and was not to be taken seriously. The ease with which he could be bribed with a giant also reduced his credibility in Europe. It is usually thought that Frederick William was unaware of the contempt in which he was held, and that the giants represented a genuine obsession of his. However, a different picture emerges from his *Political Testament*, a document ignored by most historians.

1 Throughout my life I have been careful not to draw down the envy of Austria on my head. This has forced me to pursue two passions which are really alien to me, namely unbounded avarice and an exaggerated regard for tall soldiers. Only under the
5 disguise of these spectacular eccentricities was I allowed to gather a large treasury and assemble a powerful army. Now this money and these troops lie at the disposal of my successor, who requires no such mask.

This revealing statement, written towards the end of his reign, indicates that Frederick William was aware of what Europe thought of his strange habit. Perhaps it also proves that the whole business of the tall soldiers was an elaborate charade he played on Europe to make them think he was harmless, and that in reality he had no interest in giants at all. More likely, perhaps, is the interpretation that he really did like giants, but was shrewd enough to see how his hobby could be turned to Prussia's advantage.

By his military reforms, Frederick William had created the most powerful army in Europe. In the process he had solved the problem of the nobles, and ensured the whole process was accomplished without major disruption to the economy. Moreover, he had achieved all this without arousing the fear and anger of his neighbours. It was a remarkable achievement. Yet it represented only one strand of his campaign to strengthen the Prussian state.

4 Foreign Policy

a) Peaceful Policies

For a monarch so obsessed with strengthening his state and building up the army, Frederick William's foreign policy was surprisingly pacific. Not only did he avoid wars and alliances as far as possible, but on the few occasions on which he actively pursued foreign policy aims, he did so with a singular lack of skill. Various explanations have been offered by historians for his lack of initiative in his foreign policy. The most Machiavellian explanation is that this was all part of his cunning plan to persuade Europe that the rise of the Prussian army was no threat to anyone. The more likely explanation was his awareness of his own lack of skill – he once advised his son to 'beware of imitating me in diplomacy, because I have never understood it' – and a moral objection to war – its destructiveness, its risks and its lack of justification. This is not the same thing as arguing he had no ambitions abroad. In fact he had some definite aims, but was limited by his instinctive loyalty to Austria and his reliance on diplomacy rather than war to achieve them. These aims were to obtain Swedish Pomerenia, the provinces of Julich and Berg, and (more optimistically) West Prussia (see the map on page 68).

The opportunity to achieve his first aim came early in his reign. Prussia belatedly joined the Great Northern War against Sweden in 1715. Prussian troops had no difficulty in taking Stralsund from the exhausted Swedes. Frederick William then made peace with Sweden (1720) and at last acquired West Pomerenia with its useful port of Stettin. However, Frederick William's erstwhile ally Peter I of Russia was not pleased that Prussia had dropped out of the war without consulting him. Peter accused Frederick William of wanting to go fishing without getting his boots wet – a perceptive judgement that might well be applied to his foreign policy as a whole.

The main principle underlying Frederick William's alliances was his loyalty to the Habsburgs and his acceptance of their supremacy within the Holy Roman Empire. Frederick William inherited from his father friendly relations with England (to whose king he was related) and the United Provinces (Netherlands) as well as with Austria. In general he tried to continue these policies, but when he had to choose between them in the 1720s, he opted to stay friends with Austria rather than England. 'I am more of an imperialist than a Hanoverian', he confided. This well-known loyalty to the Emperor was one reason why Charles VI ignored warnings from his advisers about the rising power of Prussia. Why go to war with a state so obviously deferential and loyal? This loyalty was seen during the War of Polish Succession (1733–8). Prussia had long coveted the Polish province of West Prussia because its acquisition would link East Prussia with Brandenburg. It might, therefore, have been expected that he would intervene in the war to promote his own interests. Instead, at Austria's request, Frederick William obediently declared war on France and sent troops to the Rhine to fight under the command of Prince Eugene. Eugene, who had been warning Austrian emperors for over thirty years to beware of the rise of Prussia, conceded that these were the best troops he had. Apart from giving Crown Prince Frederick (later Frederick the Great) his first taste of real war, Prussian involvement in the war achieved little. When the Treaty of Vienna ending the war was signed in 1738, Prussia received nothing in return for the contribution it had made.

The clearest ambition Frederick William had in foreign affairs was to acquire the small states of Julich and Berg. Prussia had dynastic claims to them that went back more than a century. Frederick William was determined to have the provinces and to use diplomacy to get them. In moves not dissimilar to Charles VI's attempts to have the Pragmatic Sanction accepted, Frederick William touted his claims around Europe during the 1720s. It was an obvious step when in 1729 Prussia accepted the Pragmatic Sanction in return for Austrian support for his claim to the two states. Austria then gradually withdrew its support. Frederick William felt betrayed. It is possible that Charles VI decided that Prussia was now becoming too strong and must not be allowed to acquire more land, trusting (correctly) that Frederick William was too loyal to go to war with him. He did, however, leave a lasting legacy of bitterness between Prussia and Austria. On one famous occasion towards the end of his reign, after commenting bitterly on Austrian treachery, Frederick William pointed to his son and said 'There is the one who will avenge me'.

b) How Successful was Frederick William's Foreign Policy?

Overall, Frederick William's foreign policy had been clumsy and unsuccessful. He gained one piece of land from a helpless Sweden, but he failed either to assert his claims in Poland when there was an opportunity, or to gain the two pieces of land he really cared about. This was one important field in which Frederick William noticeably failed to strengthen his state. Although he is often given credit for avoiding wars, he did in fact join in the only two wars affecting central Europe that occurred during his reign. Foreign envoys were dismissive – 'He is neither useful to his friends, nor dangerous to his enemies', sneered the French ambassador. Yet for all the weaknesses of his foreign policy, it was not unprincipled. In his *Political Testament*, Frederick William put forward his beliefs with a surprising passion:

1 I beg you not to begin an unjust war, because God forbids unjust wars. You must give account for every man killed in an unjust war. Look at history and you will see that nothing good ever

comes from unjust wars. This, my dear successor, demonstrates
5 the hand of God. Therefore I beg you never to start an unjust war
in order that God's blessing may lie upon you and your army. You
are, of course, lord upon earth, but you must account to God for
any blood spilt in an unjust cause. This is hard fact. Therefore,
keep your conscience clear before God, and you will have a happy
10 reign.

This passage reminds us how important religious principles were to
Frederick William. Unfortunately, a study of history suggests the
opposite of what he believed. Unjust aggression, far from being
punished by God, is often rewarded with success. Frederick William's
son would prove the point in 1740.

5 The Reform of Government

The second of the three main strands of Frederick William's work was
the reform of the system of government. He inherited a system largely
unchanged for a century. A network of local officials (*Steurräte*) existed
in the provinces to carry out the ruler's orders. They were invariably
local nobles nominated by the local estates. There were therefore some
doubts about where their real loyalty lay. In addition, there were
problems between the rival tax collectors responsible for military
income and the civilian budget. In 1722 repeated disputes between
officials persuaded Frederick William of the need for a wholesale
reform. The new system, which started in 1723, was to last virtually
unchanged for the next 80 years.

Frederick William tightly centralised government. All decisions were
made by him and his instructions were issued through a handful of
trusted secretaries who together made up the 'king and his cabinet'.
The word 'cabinet' should not be confused with the workings of the
British cabinet. The secretaries in Frederick William's cabinet were
junior officials who merely wrote and despatched their master's orders
and who summarised the numerous reports that arrived from different
parts of the state.

Under the king three committees operated which together handled
most government business (see the table on page 43). The most
important of these was the *Generaloberfinanzkriegsunddomänendirektor-
ium*, which, for convenience, is normally known in English by its its
much shortened title of General Directory. However, the full title,
although clumsy, does accurately describe its functions. This committee was responsible for finance, the economy, communications and
army administration. Its responsibilities therefore covered most, but
not all, of the work of the government. The *Justizrat* was responsible
for justice, education and religion, whilst the *Kabinetsministerium*
looked after Prussian foreign policy. All three were organised in similar

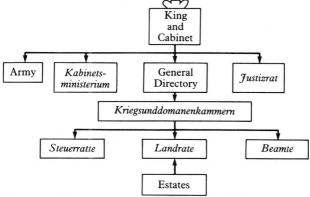

The System of Government under Frederick William I

fashion. They were committees of senior civil servants, headed by a president and vice-presidents. They were allowed no initiative themselves. They could offer advice and recommendations to the king – but only if all the members of the committee agreed. They were not allowed to take any action without the monarch's express approval. The king could, and often did, overrule the advice of his committees. The insistence on a collegiate approach and the refusal to allow his ministers and bureaucrats to take decisions on their own were designed to prevent the emergence of over-powerful courtiers whose power could threaten that of the king.

Local government was also reorganised with the division of Prussia into 17 provinces, each headed by a Provincial War Chamber. This was again a committee of civil servants responsible for collecting the taxes and developing the economy in its own area. Finally, at the lowest level, there were three types of local officials – the *Steurräte* in the towns, the *Beamte* who looked after the royal domains, and the *Landrate* in rural areas. The *Landrate*, being local nobles, were probably the only officials who enjoyed any independence from the tight royal control which was otherwise the most striking feature of the system of government.

Essential to the success of this system was the programme of supervision and inspection that Frederick William introduced. He cut salaries and demanded a total commitment from his bureaucrats. Detailed instructions, known as *Règlements*, were issued specifying their duties and hours of work. Those for the General Directory, for instance, laid down that meetings were to start at 7am in summer and 8am in winter and must continue until all business was finished. Lunch would be provided, but meetings were to continue during lunch. Anyone who arrived late without the written permission of the king was to be heavily fined. Frederick William personally toured his provinces for months at a time, descending unexpectedly to check on the work of individual bureaucrats or committees. The stories of his ruthlessness when he found people not working hard enough were legion. At the very least inefficient civil servants could expect a beating with the cane Frederick William always carried with him. At worst, he had an East Prussian councillor publicly hanged for taking bribes. In between, he had offenders imprisoned without trial. He also established a system of *Fiscals*. These were junior civil servants who spied on their fellows and sent regular reports to the king. Since nobody knew who the Fiscal was in any office, this led to an atmosphere of suspicion and fear.

Prussia was noted for its honest and hard-working civil servants. There were only 14,000 of them – a small number both by modern standards and by the standards of other eighteenth century states. Yet despite the low wages, long hours, and the spying, there was no shortage of volunteers, particularly from the middle class, for a job that offered security, status and responsibility. New departments were established at Halle University to train students for a career in government service. Yet all the time Frederick William never ceased to remind them how unimportant they were compared to soldiers. 'I have command over the army. Why should I not have command over a thousand damned pen-pushers?', was a typical remark from the monarch.

Frederick William's reform of government created a remarkably efficient and hard-working bureaucracy. Its success is seen in the smooth way it continued to function during Frederick II's wars. However, it is possible to exaggerate its benefits. Not all civil servants were honest and hard-working, despite the king's efforts. His own brutality was passed down the line, and Prussian bureaucrats were notorious for the harsh way they administered their areas. By deliberately banning any initiative, Prussian bureaucrats became as much unthinking automatons as Prussian soldiers. The system worked, and it worked well, but it was also inflexible and resistant to change. In the short run, Frederick William had significantly strengthened his state through his reform of government, but he had created a system that was too rigid to adapt to changing circumstances.

6 Finances

The third strand of Frederick William's plan to strengthen Prussia was to make her financially secure. Under Frederick I, Prussia had been reliant on foreign subsidies and had lost her freedom of action as a result. This was a situation the new king was determined to avoid in future. Frederick William relied on three main sources for his income. The Land Tax was the main tax in Prussia. In most provinces it was levied only on peasants: nobles were exempt. Around 40 per cent of a peasant's income went on this tax – a proportion that hardly changed during his reign, and one which was similar to the amount peasants paid in other states. Frederick William did manage to impose the Land Tax on the East Prussian *Junkers*. This was done not so much to raise money as to increase his control on this, the most powerful of his noble groups. In one of his most memorable statements, Frederick William explained that 'I will ruin the authority of the *Junkers* and establish sovereignity like a rock of bronze'. The second source of income was the Excise. This was a duty levied on various consumer goods, and it tended to hit the middle class and nobles most because of their higher consumption. Already levied on such staples as flour, meat, salt and tobacco, Frederick William extended it to cover luxuries such as fruit, tea and coffee. Finally, up to half of his income came from his own lands. Frederick William owned a large proportion of Prussia as Crown Domains. In the previous reign these had been rented out on long leases, but Frederick William preferred to rent them out on very short leases – usually only six years. The short leases meant that the rent could be reviewed regularly. During his reign the lands owned by the crown actually increased, since Frederick William was always willing to buy up the land of a bankrupt noble.

Frederick William also ensured that the money received was managed with the same tight supervision as his civil servants were. Court expenditure was reduced to a minimum and an Auditing Office was set up to supervise the collection and management of taxes. The results were impressive. State income roughly doubled during his reign, from $3\frac{1}{2}$ to 7 million thalers a year. Not only was he well able to afford his army, but Frederick William was also able to save substantial amounts, which were kept in strongrooms in his palace. When he died, his son inherited not just a strong government and 83,000 soldiers, but a treasure of around 8 million thalers – more than a whole year's income. Prussia was in fact the *only* state in Europe where the king regularly received more than he actually spent. This freed him from all worries about relying on foreign subsidies – or from needing to ask his own nobles to help him out. The contrast with Charles VI's financial situation is striking.

7 Religion and Population

Where Charles VI persecuted, Frederick William tolerated. This was largely practical politics. Religious toleration was already well established in Prussia, having been practised by successive rulers for nearly a century. It was necessary if immigrants were to be encouraged to come freely to build up the population. Frederick William continued the custom, and immigrants continued to enter the country. Some 20,000 Protestants fleeing from the persecutions of the Catholic Archbishop of Salzburg were settled in East Prussia where they helped repopulate districts following the outbreak of Black Death in 1709. Catholics were also welcomed, and Frederick William went so far as to establish Catholic chaplains in the army alongside the Lutheran pastors. Partly as a result of encouraging immigration, the population of his state grew steadily from around 2 million at the start of his reign to about 2½ million in 1740. Although this was still a modest figure when compared to the great powers of Europe, it did represent a significant increase in the number of potential workers and soldiers available to the king.

8 Education

Frederick William despised educated people. He starved his universities of funds. The Academies of Science and Arts fell into decline. The king used his position to sneer at intellectuals. In particular, his President of the Academy of Science, Gundling, was for several years the victim of crude practical jokes, such as finding his house walled up! When Gundling died, Frederick William had him buried in a beer barrel. When Wolff, the foremost law professor of his age, suggested that desertion from the army might not always be a capital offence, Frederick William dismissed him from his post and gave him 48 hours to leave the country. Wincklemann, another Prussian intellectual, went into exile rather than face the constant sneering of his monarch. He left one of the most picturesque, but also one of the most damning descriptions of the frustrations of an intellectual living under Frederick William. 'It was better', he proclaimed, 'to be a eunuch in a Turkish harem than a subject of the King of Prussia!'

Yet Frederick William, whose idea of relaxation was spending an evening exchanging the crudest of jokes and drinking beer with army officers in his *Tabagie* ('Tobacco Parliament'), was not quite as uninterested in education as he appeared. In 1717 he issued a decree establishing a system of state primary schools for all children aged between 5 and 12. It seems that around 1,000 schools were built during his reign. However, the achievement was not really impressive. Most of these were one-room village schools, and they were starved of funds. There was no provision for the training of teachers, nor any attempt to make school attendance compulsory.

That the decree was of limited effect is indicated by the fact that Frederick II had to start from scratch when he also tried to introduce a state education system 46 years later. Although there is no reason to doubt Frederick William's sincerity in hoping to establish a basic level of education for all Prussians, he clearly regarded it as a much lower priority than the building up of his army. To him, as to so many rulers throughout the history of Europe, soldiers were more useful than well educated citizens.

9 The Economy

Frederick William took a paternalistic line on the economy. He followed the mercantilist policies which were popular at the time. This involved encouraging industry and exports and discouraging imports, in an attempt to build up a healthy trade surplus with other states. He mainly used the excise duties to achieve this, by putting heavy taxes on imported goods. From time to time he banned certain goods entirely. For example, he banned the export of Prussian wool in order to force farmers to sell their wool cheaply to Prussian textile manufacturers and so encourage this new (to Prussia) industry. He took action to reduce the power of the guilds in towns, in particular persuading the Imperial Diet to pass a decree ending the rights of journeymen. These were skilled workers who had been trained and passed examinations set by the guilds. Until Frederick William's initiative, only journeymen were allowed to practise certain crafts, and this prevented outsiders from starting factories or opening shops. Thanks to Frederick William's decree, the guilds lost their monopoly on trade and industry. There was a modest industrial expansion during his reign, notably in industries connected with the army, such as textiles and munitions. On the other hand, the luxury industries, such as porcelain and tapestries, patronised by his father, collapsed during the reign.

Overall, it is difficult to discern any great progress made in the economy between 1713 and 1740. Frederick William's officials, although attempting to encourage industry and trade through decrees, were probably doing more harm than good since they stifled individual initiative. The small size of the middle class, the fact that towns were ruled by royal officials rather than by their citizens, and the continued existence of serfdom (resulting in a shortage of labour in the towns) all played their part in hampering any dramatic economic progress. In economic affairs Frederick William achieved no more than Charles VI.

It was a similar story with serfdom. Frederick William was aware of the hardships that serfs endured, but he was also aware that he needed the serfs' income for his taxes and their bodies for his army. Although frequent laws were passed to protect them – they were not to be worked more than two days a week and could not be punished by their masters – and although these laws were generally enforced on crown lands, they were widely ignored on noble lands. Frederick William, aware of his increasing reliance on the nobility, made few efforts to ensure compliance there. In any case, the local officials responsible for ensuring the laws were obeyed, the *Steurräte*, were themselves nobles who had everything to lose if these laws were enforced too effectively. There were limits to what even this, the most absolute of eighteenth century absolute monarchs, could expect to be able to impose on his nobles.

10 Assessment

Frederick William had never enjoyed good health. From an early age he was afflicted by a variety of illnesses, including gout, piles, migraines, boils and stomach cramps. Later in life he developed dropsy, which made him so fat that it took four men to lift him on to his horse. His illnesses may have all been symptoms of porphyria, the rare inherited disease from which, it has since been discovered, a number of inter-related monarchs may have been suffering. These illnesses always threatened to cut his life short, and as early as 1722, when he was only 34, his life was being despaired of. Certainly his constant illnesses did nothing to improve his always short temper. His final illness and death in 1740 were conducted in characteristic style. He ordered that his coffin be brought into his bedroom in readiness and he made careful arrangements for his funeral. He had an abdication document prepared, in case he survived but was incapable of ruling any longer. When the mourners sang a line from one of his favourite hymns, 'Naked I came into the world, naked I shall leave it', he woke out of his coma to protest 'That's not true. I'll be wearing my uniform'. Amongst his last words were 'I have put the state and army in order'. This phrase accurately sums up both his aims and his achievements.

Although only one biography of Frederick William in English has been written this century, many writers have attempted to assess his reign and importance. The first noteworthy judgement came from the man who knew him best, his own son, Frederick II. His judgement has had considerable influence on those of later historians.

1 What a terrible man, but what a just man, and intelligent and fitted for state affairs! You have no idea of the thorough order he put into all branches of the government. There never was a prince more capable of entering into the smallest details in order to bring
5 all parts of the state to the greatest degree of perfection. It is therefore through his care, his endless labour, his great economies, and the severe discipline he brought to the army he created, that it has been possible for me to do what I have done.

This judgement – that Frederick William was a brutal but great man who made Frederick II's achievements possible – has been echoed by many historians since. Lord Acton, for instance, described him as 'the Peter the Great of Prussia'. Others have described him as 'the father of the Prussian bureaucracy', 'the maker of the Prussian state', and the man who 'made Prussia a state capable of greatness'. These flattering comments reached their apogee in Nazi Germany when Hitler's historians praised Frederick William as a prototype Nazi. They ignored his religious toleration and encouragement to foreign immigrants, but the adulation he received in the 1930s is a good example of how each generation tends to mould its historical heroes in the image of contemporary politics.

Admirers of Frederick William point out how he saved his country from bankruptcy and created a modern and efficient state with a powerful army and sound finances. He was a man interested in the realities of power, yet was wise enough not to use the army more than necessary. In addition, he showed great skill in persuading the rest of Europe, and Austria in particular, that Prussia was no threat.

However, not all comments have been so favourable. 'He was merely a grotesque Seargeant-Major', claimed Eyck, whilst a particularly virulent attack came from the skilled pen of the nineteenth century historian, Macaulay.

1 His character was disfigured by odious vices, and whose eccentricities have never before been seen outside a madhouse. His mind was so ill-regulated that all his inclinations became passions, and all his passions became moral and intellectual disease.

Historians have criticised Frederick William for his cruelty, both to his subjects and to the people around him. In particular, his brutal treatment of his own son Frederick, corrupting a sensitive and intelligent boy, has been attacked. The effects of an unhappy childhood on the later policies of Frederick II is discussed in the companion volume in the Access to History series, *Europe and the Enlightened Despots*. Historians have also commented on the excessive militarisation of Prussia, citing the 80 per cent of taxes spent on the army, and the way that army officers held many of the senior positions in government. The stifling of any initiative by civil servants and ministers has also been criticised. The lack of success in foreign policy and the failure to do much to help the serfs, the economy or education, complete a picture of a monarch who was only successful when he was brutal, and whose survival owed more to favourable circumstances than any skill on his part.

One myth can be scotched at once. It is the idea that Frederick II's achievements have unfairly overshadowed those of Frederick William. In reality most historians have gone to the other extreme, putting great emphasis on the achievements of Frederick William as the 'founder of Prussia', and ignoring those of both Frederick I and the Great Elector. It is of course true that Frederick II could never have turned Prussia into a great power without the groundwork of his father. This was freely acknowledged at the time by Frederick II. It is also true that Frederick II's own successes led historians to re-evaluate the contribution of his father to the Prussian state. Frederick William's reign is considered successful and important because of the use Frederick II made of his inheritance. It was Frederick II who by his actions drew attention to his father's achievements. Is it reasonable to claim that one was more important than the other, or would it be better to maintain that they complemented each other?

Frederick William had worked hard to strengthen the Prussian state, and had achieved notable success in creating a stable financial base, a strong if bureaucratic system of government, and a large and well-trained army. He had shown some skill in handling the *Junkers*, although at the price of giving them a powerful role in state organisations. When compared to Charles VI, he had fewer problems to face, but had shown far more determination and success in dealing with them. However, there is a danger in any approach which sees only good coming out of his reign. Clearly there were failures as well as achievements. His foreign policy was clumsy and unsuccessful. It needs to be remembered that foreign leaders were *right* to see him as an easily manipulated king. Frederick I had accepted bribes, disguised as 'subsidies' from foreign states. Frederick William, who was just as easily bribed with giants, could not expect to be treated with more respect. At home he did little to develop the economy, or education, or to help the serfs. He created an excellent army, but even here there were shortcomings, especially with the cavalry. Above all, by creating a bureaucracy which was allowed no initiative; by insisting on total obedience to orders from above; by setting an example of brutality and encouraging his subordinates to do likewise; and by creating a hybrid system which combined autocracy with bureacracy, but which relied totally on the hard work and dedication of the monarch for success, he saddled Prussia with a system of government and an attitude towards and by bureaucrats which was to have unfortunate consequences 70 years later when a rigid and unthinking regime fell easy prey to Napoleon.

There is no doubt that Frederick William was a vitally important ruler in the history of Prussia. His impact continued to be felt long after he died. He was responsible both for creating a new Prussian state able to take on and defeat the strongest powers in Europe, but also for creating those shortcomings in the system of government which would ensure its ultimate downfall.

Making notes on 'Frederick William I'

As you read the chapter, try to identify i) the problems faced by the kings of Prussia, ii) the reforms introduced by Frederick William, iii) which problems he solved, which remained unsolved and which problems (if any) actually got worse, and iv) the strengths and weaknesses of Prussia in 1740. Any discussion of the achievements of Frederick William should centre around the extent to which he had solved Prussia's problems by 1740. The following headings and questions should help guide your notes on this topic.

1 Frederick William: The Early Years. What were the strengths and weaknesses of Prussia in 1713?
2 Frederick William's philosophy. What were his aims as ruler?
3 The Army
a) In what ways did Frederick William reform the army?
b) What were the strengths and weaknesses of the Prussian army in 1740?
4 Foreign Policy
a) What were Frederick William's aims in foreign policy?
b) Why was he so unsuccessful?

For each of the following sections on domestic policy, identify i) what Frederick William did and ii) how successful his actions were.
5 Government
6 Finance
7 Religion
8 Education
9 The Economy
10 Assessment: Summarise the strengths and weaknesses of Prussia in 1740.

Answering essay questions on 'Frederick William I'

Essay questions on Frederick William often ask for a comparison between him and Frederick II. Such questions will be discussed on page 125. Questions on Frederick William alone are relatively rare. Often they are of the 'challenging statement' variety. These are questions where the examiner puts forward a particular point of view usually (but not always) in the form of a quotation, as in these examples:

1 Do you agree that for Frederick William I 'foreign policy was the least of his interests'?
2 'I find pleasure in nothing in the world except a strong army'. In what ways did this preference influence the domestic policies of Frederick William I?
3 'His achievements for Prussia were solid but unspectacular, and therefore generally undervalued.' Do you agree with this comment on the work of Frederick William I?

The first task when faced with a 'challenging statement' question is to try to untangle it. You will need to decide:

a) Which aspects of the reign you need to cover. Is this an essay which requires coverage of both domestic and foreign policy, or is it limited to particular areas?

b) What particular line or argument the examiner is putting forward.

Of course it is vital that you concentrate your answer on the particular issues raised, rather than writing a general essay about the events of the reign. Nothing is more likely to ensure that you are awarded only minimum marks than ignoring the particular question posed by the examiner and simply writing 'all you know' on Frederick William.

Question 3 may appear the most daunting, so it might be helpful to analyse what the examiner is looking for in some detail. First, does it cover all aspects of his reign, or limit you to dealing with domestic policy? When you have worked this out, the next step is to disentangle the questions the examiner wants you to answer. There are in fact four related questions being asked here. They are:

- Were Frederick William's achievements *solid*? [ie, did they last]
- Were they unspectacular?
- Have they been generally undervalued? [and if so, by whom?]
- If his achievements have been undervalued, is this because they were 'unspectacular', or might there be other reasons why he has been undervalued?

The only purpose of this untangling exercise is to identify which questions you need to answer. It does *not* mean you have to answer each question separately and to write four miniature essays in the time allowed! More realistic would be to set out to answer two questions, formed by combining the questions you have identified into groups. These groupings of questions might, for example, be:

1) Is it true to say that his achievements were solid and unspectacular?

2) Is it true they have been undervalued? If so, who has undervalued Frederick William and why?

You are now ready to prepare your answer. Which aspects of his reign give you the best examples of his work being 'solid' and 'unspectacular'? These will give you your paragraph headings. Are there any aspects which were not solid or unspectacular? You might wish to mention these, but in general you will probably find yourself agreeing with this part of the challenging statement.

The second question is less clear cut. Who exactly did 'undervalue' him? Is it, in fact, true that he has been undervalued? You should not be afraid to criticise the implications of the examiner's question, provided you have evidence to support the contention that he has not been undervalued. Where there is clear evidence that at least one person underrated Frederick William (who is that?), you need to discuss why he did so.

'Challenging statement' essay titles often worry candidates. In fact they are often easier than apparently straightforward questions because they cover less ground and ask specific questions. An example of an apparently more straightforward but actually much wider-ranging question is:

4 Consider the importance of the reign of Frederick William I in the history of Prussia.

This is an apparently easy question simply asking what his importance was. In fact, there is a sting in its tail. It is the phrase 'in the history of Prussia'. In order to answer this question properly, Frederick William would have to be compared with the rulers who came before and after him. Only by comparing his achievements with theirs can you come to an overall assessment of how important he was in the building up of the Prussian state. Although Frederick I and Frederick II are not mentioned in the title, they must be discussed as well. Since Frederick William only has been identified by name, it would be reasonable to spend most of the essay describing his importance, but a significant number of marks will be reserved by the examiner for the comparison.

Source based questions on 'Frederick William'

1 Frederick William's philosophy
Carefully read the extracts on page 34 and Frederick William's letter on page 35. Answer the following questions.
a) Who were i) 'the prince of Anhalt' (page 34 line 1) and ii) 'Fritz' (page 35 line 1)? *(2 marks)*
b) Explain why Frederick William was particularly concerned that Fritz should ignore 'vanities but stick to reality' (page 35 lines 5–6)? *(2 marks)*
c) What did Frederick William mean by 'I am the finance minister and field marshal of Prussia' (page 34 lines 1–2)? *(1 mark)*
d) What do these sources indicate about i) Frederick William's religious principles, and, ii) his attitude towards his people? *(4 marks)*
e) Which of the aims described in these sources did he achieve, and which did he fail to achieve? *(6 marks)*

2 Frederick William's testament
Carefully read the two extracts from Frederick William's testament on pages 39 and 41–2. Answer the following questions.
a) Explain what is meant by 'lord upon earth' (page 42 line 7) *(2 marks)*
b) Why, according to Frederick William, were unjust wars always wrong? *(4 marks)*
c) What do these extracts suggest about i) Frederick William's religious principles, and, ii) his attitude towards Austria? *(4 marks)*

d) How convincing is Frederick William's explanation for his obsession with money and giants? Justify your answer. *(5 marks)*

e) Political testaments were often written at this time as advice from a monarch to his successor. Of what value are testaments such as this to a historian? *(5 marks)*

3 Assessments of Frederick William

Carefully read the judgements on Frederick William by Frederick II on page 48 and by Macaulay on page 49. Answer the following questions.

a) In what ways do Frederick II and Macaulay agree in their assessment of Frederick William? *(4 marks)*

b) In what ways do they disagree? *(4 marks)*

c) Is it reasonable to say that Frederick II's judgement must be rejected because, as Frederick William's son, he was biased in his father's favour? Use the extract to support your answer. *(6 marks)*

d) 'Neither of these sources presents a convincing picture of Frederick William'. Use the sources and your own knowledge to discuss this statement. *(6 marks)*

CHAPTER 4

Habsburgs versus Hohenzollerns

1 The Outbreak of War

Europe was used to wars in the eighteenth century. It was the usual method by which monarchs settled quarrels with their neighbours. The ruler of a great power expected to go to war several times during his reign, both to defend and to extend his possessions. A monarch such as Frederick William I, who consciously attempted to avoid war, was treated as an eccentric. Nevertheless, when the young Frederick II decided to launch an attack on the Austrian Empire in December 1740, it caught Europe totally by surprise. Both the causes of his decision and the effects of it have been a matter of controversy amongst historians ever since.

Frederick's decision to go to war with Austria appears to have been made casually. Certainly there was neither any hesitation about his decision, nor any attempt to discuss the wisdom of such a move. Charles VI had died suddenly and unexpectedly on 20 October 1740. Eight days later Frederick told his senior advisers of his decision to go to war in an attempt to conquer the rich Austrian province of Silesia which bordered Prussia. The next weeks were spent in preparing the army in great secrecy, and in trying to establish some legal claim to Silesia. The secrecy was so great that not even Prince Leopold of Anhalt-Dessau, the veteran commander of the Prussian army, was informed until after the invasion had begun. When the Prussian army did cross into Silesia on 14 December 1740 surprise was total. The Austrians were completely unprepared for the onslaught and had neither troops nor fortresses in Silesia in any state to resist the attack. Within a month it was all over. The tiny Austrian garrisons surrendered without a fight. Even the main city, Breslau, fell after a token three-day siege. Austria's most valuable province had been conquered in a campaign of lightning speed and with the loss of just one Prussian soldier – accidentally drowned. Rarely in history has such a long and bloody war started so easily and cheaply.

The Prussian conquest of Silesia raises a number of questions. What were Frederick's real reasons for attacking the province? Why were the Austrians caught so much by surprise? Why did Frederick's attack so quickly involve the rest of Europe in a general war?

a) The Decision to Attack

Frederick had a number of reasons for attacking Silesia when he did. His foreign minister obediently extracted some obscure legal claims to part of Silesia, but Frederick cheerfully admitted that these were put forward purely as propaganda. Frederick never pretended that he had any real legal right to the province. His reasons had far more to do with practical politics than legality.

Firstly, Frederick wished to see Prussia become a great power. With its poor resources and low population, this could only be done through conquest. Silesia was an ideal target. Geographically linked with Prussia (although its conquest would give Frederick even longer borders to defend), it was economically valuable. Its population of one million, its well developed agriculture and industry, and its large coal and iron deposits would all bring immediate benefit to Prussia. Furthermore, there was every expectation that the people of Silesia would not oppose, and might actually welcome, Prussian rule because many of them were Protestant and had suffered persecution under Charles VI. In the event, most Silesians did indeed transfer their loyalty to Prussia despite having been part of the Austrian Empire for over two hundred years. The religious intolerance of successive Austrian rulers now rebounded on them.

The second factor was the ideal timing. We will never know whether Frederick would have risked attacking Silesia if Charles VI had lived on. Charles's death gave him a perfect opportunity to attack whilst Austria was adjusting to the rule of a new, young, inexperienced and female ruler. Frederick was also fortunate that Empress Anna of Russia had died in the same month as Charles. Russia, which had been an ally of Austria since 1726, was plunged into chaos for several months and would be unable to help Austria. Immediate action was essential if Prussia were to succeed with its robbery. Within a few months Maria Theresa would be firmly established. If Frederick were to have any chance of keeping Silesia, he had to take it whilst the Austrians were at their weakest.

There were other, personal, factors in Frederick's decision to attack at this time, and he was honest enough to admit them to his friends.

 1 Who would have thought that destiny has chosen a poet to topple
   the political system of Europe and to turn upside down the
   political combinations of its rulers ... My youthfulness, the
   burning embers of my passion, my thirst for fame, even curiosity
 5 have torn me from the joys of tranquility. The satisfaction of
   seeing my name in the gazettes [newspapers] and later in history
   books seduced me.

In similar vein he wrote to another friend:

The possession of troops trained and ready for war; a well filled treasury and a lively temperament ... Ambition and the desire to make a name for myself.

It has been suggested by some historians that there was also an element of revenge in his decision. He was determined to show Europe that he was not another Frederick William, easily ignored or manipulated by great powers. The influence of Frederick William is also evident in the cynicism of Frederick's unprovoked aggression. Frederick William's harsh upbringing of his son had succeeded only too well in driving away the idealism of his youth. Frederick, who had once written that aggressive wars were always wrong, now believed that the ends justified the means.

However, although it need not be doubted that Frederick did have some personal motives of wanting both fame and revenge, it is certain that his main motive was the wish to increase Prussian land and power and to seize a favourable opportunity, as he explained frankly in a memorandum to his ministers.

1 Silesia is the portion of the Empire to which we have the strongest claim and which is the most suitable for the House of Brandenburg. It is just to maintain one's rights and to seize the opportunity of the Emperor's death to take it. The superiority of our troops
5 and their speed, in a word the advantage we have over our neighbours, gives us in this unexpected emergency a superiority over the other powers of Europe. If we wait for Saxony or Bavaria to start war, we could not prevent the former gaining land which is contrary to our interests . . . We must occupy Silesia before
10 winter and then negotiate. When we are in possession we can negotiate with success. We would never get anything but trifles by merely negotiating.

Was Frederick justified in attacking Silesia? It is easy to criticise his action on moral grounds. Frederick attacked a neighbour who had done him no harm. He seized a province to which he had no legal claim simply because it would be useful to Prussia and in order to make himself famous. He deliberately chose the moment when Austria was at its weakest, and attacked her without any formal declaration of war at the same time as his envoys were assuring Maria Theresa of his goodwill and friendship. His actions not only provoked a lengthy war, but, by their eventual success, encouraged other rulers to adopt the same ruthless and amoral attitude towards their weaker neighbours.

A generation taught to believe that wars should only be fought as a last resort after all peaceful methods have been exhausted, and then only in self-defence, will find it easy to condemn Frederick's actions, but it may not be appropriate to judge him by the supposed standards of twentieth century international relations. According to the standards of his time, Frederick was acting reasonably. His unprovoked aggression was by no means unique in eighteenth century Europe. A similar event had occured exactly forty years before when a formidable coalition of states had suddenly attacked Sweden because it was ruled by the inexperienced Charles XII, thus provoking the Great Northern War. Had France suddenly attacked Austria in 1740 this would not have aroused the same surprise since Austria and France were old enemies. Frederick's actions have aroused so much controversy because he was (supposedly) the ruler of a second-rate power taking on one of the Great Powers of Europe, and because he beat the other powers at their own game. The problem was not that Frederick was less moral than the other rulers of Europe; he was just more successful.

b) Austria's Weakness

Maria Theresa was caught completely off guard by Frederick's attack. Although the new empress was aware that her throne was insecure, an attack from Prussia was the last thing she expected. To be sure, although the provincial diets within Austria had accepted her as their new ruler without trouble, she could not be sure that other European powers would honour their commitments to the Pragmatic Sanction. The most obvious enemy was France, whose Chief Minister, Fleury, was under strong pressure from a group of ambitious and belligerent nobles led by Marshal Belle-Isle to take action to support the Bavarian claim to the Austrian throne. France was Austria's traditional enemy, a state which had only recently and reluctantly acceded to the Pragmatic Sanction, and one where many voices called for revenge for the defeats in the war of Spanish Succession. It was understandable that Austrian eyes were turned to the real danger of a joint invasion by France and Bavaria, perhaps supported by Spain. By contrast, there seemed little reason to worry about Prussia. Here was a state with no claim on the Austrian throne, traditionally loyal to the Habsburgs, and with a poetry-loving monarch who was nearly as new and insecure on his throne as Maria Theresa was on hers. It is no wonder that Maria Theresa felt confident about leaving Silesia virtually undefended and concentrating her armies against the more obvious threat. Maria Theresa could not know that Fleury was, for the time being, successfully resisting the calls for war inside his country. He preferred to await events. Maria Theresa's understandable mistake in assuming that the immediate danger came from France was to make Frederick's conquest easy.

2 The First Silesian War

a) The Battle of Mollwitz

With Silesia bloodlessly conquered, Frederick was confident enough to return to Berlin in time for Christmas. He now made an offer to Maria Theresa. If she would agree to let him keep Silesia, he would in return give her an alliance, his support for Francis (Maria Theresa's husband) as Holy Roman Emperor, and the abandonment of all other Prussian claims on Austrian territory. Frederick claimed that 'I have no other purpose than the preservation of the House of Austria'.

Maria Theresa promptly and understandably rejected the proposal and prepared an army to recover her lost province. This was a courageous action on her part, since the loss of Silesia had exposed Austrian weakness to the whole of Europe. There were now ominous signs that other states might soon attack her, if only to ensure that Prussia would not be the only state to come away with spoils. In these circumstances, to have accepted Frederick's offer would have been a humiliating admission both of loss of land, and of dependence on Prussia. It might well have encouraged, rather than deterred, other states from attacking her.

Did Frederick seriously think Maria Theresa would accept such an insolent offer from the highwayman who had just robbed her? It seems that he probably did. Frederick generally despised women, and perhaps assumed that Maria Theresa would be as easily bullied as his own wife. Events were to show that he had underrated Maria Theresa's courage and determination, although not her power.

* The Prussian and Austrian armies met at Mollwitz in April 1741. The fate not just of Silesia depended on the outcome. An Austrian victory might have led both to the recovery of the lost province and to the deterring of others from trying to follow Prussia's example. It was therefore a double disaster for Austria that the Prussians narrowly won the battle. Little of the credit for this victory should go to Frederick, who fled the battlefield convinced that the battle was lost. But even without their commander, the steady and well-trained Prussian infantry defeated the Austrian attack. The battle tells us nothing about Frederick's military skill, but a great deal about the high quality of the Prussian army. It was not so much Frederick's first victory as Frederick William's last victory.

The Battle of Mollwitz was one of the decisive battles in eighteenth century European history. Although it was a small battle by later standards, with about 20,000 men on each side, it ensured that Prussia would keep Silesia. It also made it certain that the war would spread more widely.

b) The Intervention of France

Until April 1741 there was a possibility that other European states would keep out of the war between Austria and Prussia. Certainly Fleury, in control of French foreign policy, was still urging the headstrong Louis XV to be cautious. However, Mollwitz put irrestistible pressure on both France and other states. Prussia's victory had been unexpected. The fact that a supposed second-rate power could so easily conquer Silesia and then defeat the Austrian army seemed to prove that the Austrian Empire was about to collapse. Now it was essential to join the war and take a share of the spoils.

In May 1741 a reluctant Fleury was obliged to support Bavaria's claim to the Austrian throne and to prepare for war. Within a few weeks Spain and Saxony had joined the alliance, and France had made a formal alliance with Prussia. These developments in turn drove England, already at war with Spain, into an alliance with Austria. This alliance was not caused, as is sometimes claimed, because the British government were appalled at the combined attack on an innocent and helpless ruler, but because of the coincidence that both Austria and England were at war with the same state.

In theory the allies – France, Prussia, Spain, Saxony and Bavaria – were united in their aims. Prussia was to keep Silesia and Saxony was to gain the neighbouring province of Moravia. France and Spain were to make (unspecified) territorial gains from Austria. The rump of the Empire was to be given to Elector Charles of Bavaria who, the allies now decided, was the rightful ruler of Austria after all. These states, on the surface, represented a formidable coalition against Austria. Events would soon prove that they had little in common except a wish to take as much as possible for themselves.

3 The War of Austrian Succession

During 1740 there had been two separate wars in Europe: the War of Jenkins' Ear between Britain and Spain, which was a colonial and trade war beginning in 1739, and the Silesian War between Austria and Prussia. It was French intervention which resulted in the two wars combining into a single war usually known as the War of Austrian Succession (1741–8).

For some months Maria Theresa's situation appeared critical. She had already lost Silesia, and now had to face invasion from her other enemies. In August 1741 a French army, commanded by Marshal Belle-Isle, combined with the Bavarians and invaded Austria. This was followed by the Bavarian conquest of Bohemia. In 1742 Charles of Bavaria was elected Holy Roman Emperor – the first non-Habsburg Emperor in over 300 years. The total collapse of Austria appeared imminent.

The impression was misleading. Maria Theresa was saved by a number of factors, including her own determination, the support she gained from Hungary, the mistakes of Marshal Belle-Isle, and the machinations of Frederick. The support of the Hungarian Diet, obtained after an emotional appeal to the nobles to save the empire, provided Maria Theresa with a much needed army, but this would have appeared too late to save her empire, had not an over-confident

Belle-Isle chosen to capture Prague rather than the more important Vienna.

Ironically, the greatest contribution to Maria Theresa's survival came from her most dangerous enemy, Frederick. It is necessary to understand why Frederick adopted his complicated policy towards Maria Theresa. Frederick had been hoping for a short and limited war. He had no wish to see Austrian power replaced by that of France or Bavaria. It was, therefore, in his interests to ensure that the Austrian Empire survived, as long as it did not become strong enough to reconquer Silesia. To achieve this would require considerable diplomatic skill, and it was to this new area of activity that Frederick now turned his attention.

As early as October 1741 Frederick negotiated a truce with Austria, the Treaty of Klein-Schnellendorf. This enabled him to rest his army, whilst it offered Maria Theresa a chance to concentrate her energies on defeating the more immediately dangerous enemies of France and Bavaria. This action was a flagrant breach of the treaty of alliance Frederick had made with France only a few months previously: the allies were starting to learn, as Maria Theresa had already done, that the King of Prussia was not to be trusted. The Austrians seized their opportunity and invaded Bavaria, capturing Munich itself in February 1742.

This unexpectedly swift Austrian revival alarmed Frederick, who saw that it would only be a matter of time before Maria Theresa again attempted to recapture Silesia. He accordingly re-entered the war in the spring of 1742 and defeated the Austrians at the Battle of Chotusitz (May 1742). Once again this victory was due more to the skill and determination of the Prussian soldiers than to any quality of Frederick's. Austria came under strong pressure from her ally, Britain, to try to reduce the number of enemies facing her. Therefore, a reluctant Maria Theresa, with no prospect of recovering Silesia in the near future, agreed to a formal peace treaty with Frederick.

The Treaty of Berlin (July 1742) confirmed the Prussian occupation of Silesia. In return for this, Prussia dropped out of the war. Once again Frederick had dismayed his supposed allies and had enabled Austria to concentrate on fighting France and Bavaria. Frederick was again given time to rest his army and to rebuild his finances. He could not assume that Maria Theresa had given up Silesia for good, and planned to be well prepared should it be necessary to resume fighting.

As in 1741, Maria Theresa demonstrated that, whilst her generals might not be able to defeat Frederick, they were competent enough to defeat the French and Bavarians. During 1742 the French and Bavarians were driven out of Bohemia. In 1743 Bavaria was forced to drop out of the war. Great Britain, which was not yet formally at war with France, gave useful assistance to Austria by defeating a French army at Dettingen in 1743 – a battle famous in British history for being the last time a British monarch (George II) commanded the army in person. By 1744 Maria Theresa was confident, not only of saving her Empire, but of defeating the French and gaining some territory – possibly Alsace and Lorraine.

These developments alarmed Frederick who assumed that Austria was now strong enough to consider attempting to recapture Silesia. Another pre-emptive strike was therefore required, and in characteristic style he acted alone and without warning. He justified his renewal of war with a statement to the courts of Europe which shows that he was prepared to use propaganda to support his foreign policy.

1 The King feels obliged to inform Europe of the plan which the present situation compels him to adopt for the welfare and tranquility of Europe. His Majesty, being unable to witness with indifference the troubles which are desolating Germany, and after
5 fruitlessly trying every means of conciliation, finds himself driven to employ the forces which God has put at his disposal to bring back peace, law and order ... in a word the King asks for nothing, and his personal interests are not in question. He only takes up arms to restore liberty to the Empire, dignity to the
10 Emperor, and tranquility to Europe.

His invasion of Bohemia (August 1744) was much less successful than his two earlier attacks on Austria. The French, who had promised to help him, did nothing and left him to fight the Austrians alone. For the first time since 1741 he had to face the Austrian army alone. This time, however, the enemy he faced was more experienced and was commanded by the competent Prince Charles of Lorraine. In addition, Saxony, jealous of Prussian success, had switched sides and sent 30,000 soldiers to help the Austrians. The Prussians were driven out of Bohemia, suffering a high desertion rate because of the cold weather. The Austrians were at last convinced that they could defeat their outnumbered enemy.

It was now that Frederick's abilities as a general first showed themselves. He had learned much from the campaigns of the previous years, and he put this into practice when he defeated the much larger Austrian army twice, at Hohenfriedburg (May 1745) and Sohr (September 1745). Both these victories owed as much to Frederick's innovative tactics as they did to the traditional fighting qualities of the Prussian army. Frederick was right to feel proud of these victories. For the first time he could take personal credit for Prussian success, and once again he had ensured that Prussia would keep Silesia. It was after these two unexpected victories that his nickname 'the Great' began to be used in Prussia, but it did not become more widely used until two equally stunning victories in a later war.

Maria Theresa, also facing defeats in Italy, was obliged to come to terms with Frederick. At the Treaty of Dresden (December 1745), Frederick was again confirmed in his possession of Silesia. Saxony had to pay Prussia a million thalers as the price for backing the wrong side. In return, Prussia recognised the election of Francis, Maria Theresa's husband, as the new Holy Roman Emperor following the death of Charles of Bavaria in 1744.

For Frederick II, the War of Austrian Succession was over. He continued to observe the war carefully, but it became clear that as Austria and France fought each other to exhaustion, Austria would not be in a position to renew her attack on Silesia. The war between Austria and France dragged on until 1748. Both countries were determined to gain something for all the effort they had put in. Unlike Prussia, they had been at war with each other continuously since 1741. In the colonies too, Britain continued to fight with both France and Spain, but little land changed hands.

By 1748 both Austria and France were facing bankruptcy. There was also, perhaps, a growing awareness in both countries that they were fighting the wrong enemy. The one state which had clearly benefited from the war was enjoying the fruits of peace and exploiting the resources of its new province. It was time for the two old rivals to cut their losses. Encouraged by Britain, serious peace talks opened at Aix-la-Chapelle in 1748.

4 The Treaty of Aix-la-Chapelle

The treaty that was signed in October 1748 was a truce of exhaustion, not a peace treaty. None of the issues which had developed during the war were settled, and it was clear from the start that another war was likely to break out once the rivals had recovered their strength. The terms of the treaty can be briefly summarised. All states returned the territory they had conquered during the war, apart from some small pieces of land in Italy, so that no significant gains or losses were made by any of the warring states. In addition, France recognised the Hanoverian dynasty in Britain, thus abandoning its long-standing but unrealistic support of the Jacobite pretenders to the throne.

Prussia, which took no part in the treaty, having made peace in 1745, had emerged as the only winner from the War of Austrian Succession. Frederick, through a combination of military skill, luck, ruthlessness and skilful diplomacy, had achieved all his objectives. He had gained the valuable province of Silesia, had fought for much less time than the other combatants, had conserved his state's finances, and had defeated Austria while at the same time ensuring that Austria, rather than France, would continue as the major power in Germany. It was a remarkable achievement, but the political cost had been high. Frederick now found that other leaders distrusted and feared him.

One overriding problem remained in 1748 that would ensure that this treaty would only be a truce, not a peace. Maria Theresa would not accept the loss of Silesia and from the moment the treaty was signed, she started to work towards the recovery of her lost province. Frederick never doubted that Maria Theresa would try to regain Silesia once her finances and army were restored, but was confident that he could defeat her again in war if necessary. If another war in Europe took place, it was certain that France, still considered the pre-eminent state in Europe, would once more participate.

The question French leaders had to address was which country to fight. Who posed the greatest threat to French interests? Was it Austria, the traditional rival, or Britain who threatened French colonies and trade? There was also another possibility. France might decide that Prussia, which had proved so unreliable an ally in the recent war, actually posed a greater threat to her interests than either Britain or Austria. France's tragedy was that she was ruled by a king, Louis XV, who lacked any clear aims in foreign affairs and who, despite the experience of the recent war, still felt that his country was strong enough to fight as many enemies as it liked at any one time.

5 The Diplomatic Revolution

a) Maria Theresa's Aims

Maria Theresa's determination to regain Silesia made another war with Prussia inevitable. Her motives were understandable, but were they justified? Why did she not accept the loss of Silesia? It was not, after all, the first time that Austria had lost land to an enemy. There were, in fact, a number of reasons why Maria Theresa dared not accept the loss. The most important of these was that she had lost the province, not to a foreign power such as France or the Ottoman Empire, but to a state within the Holy Roman Empire. If Austria were to retain its leadership of the Empire, it was essential that she demonstrate her ability to punish states which challenged her authority. The election of a non-Habsburg emperor in 1742, although it had only been for three years, had been an indication of how little the traditional loyalty of the electors could be relied upon if Austria were seen to be weak. In addition, Silesia was too valuable a province to lose. Nor should the religious dimension of the issue be underrated. Maria Theresa was a sincere Roman Catholic who deplored the fact that 'her' Silesians were now being ruled by Protestants. In short, her perception was that Austria could not retain its leadership of Germany, its status as a great power or its credibility as a defender of the Catholic faith as long as Prussia was seen to have got away with its blatant robbery.

It is usual to praise Maria Theresa's courage and determination in her struggle for survival and then in her efforts to regain Silesia. But it is also possible to argue that between 1748 and 1755 this courage turned to obstinacy, and that she may have overrated the damage the loss of Silesia had done to her prestige. European leaders were more inclined to take note of Austria's survival against all the odds in the recent war. Far from being discredited by the loss of Silesia, Austria was now being treated with respect for not having lost more territory. In 1748 both Britain and Russia were her allies, while Prussia showed no inclination to try to take any more land from her. Nevertheless, Maria Theresa never doubted that it was essential for Austria's survival that Silesia be reconquered. The question was how was this to be achieved?

b) The Rise of Kaunitz

The years between 1748 and 1755 were dominated by diplomatic manoeuvrings between the great powers as they jockeyed for position and allies for the forthcoming war. In some ways the second war was likely to be a repeat of the previous one. The two major sources of conflict remained unchanged: the struggle for colonial supremacy between Britain and France and the struggle for Silesia between Austria and Prussia. Most leaders, including Frederick himself, expected that once more Britain would line up with Austria, and that France would ally with Prussia. He considered Franco-Austrian hostility to be so deep-rooted that there could be no question of these two states becoming allies. It was an understandable assumption, given the previous history of the two powers, but it was to prove complacent and incorrect. Frederick, who had proved in the previous war that he was capable of conducting skilled (if unscrupulous) diplomacy, now found that his skills could not match those of the rising Austrian diplomat, Count Anton von Kaunitz.

Kaunitz had first become prominent as the Austrian delegate to the peace conference at Aix-la-Chapelle. As early as 1749 Maria Theresa had made it clear to her advisers that she intended to fight Frederick again and had asked for suggestions about how to create the most favourable combination of allies against Prussia. While her other advisers could only suggest the continuation of friendship with Britain, Kaunitz proposed something far bolder – an alliance with France. On the face of it the proposal was implausible. After all, France and Austria had been enemies for much of the previous three hundred years, and most of the wars in that period had centred around the struggle for supremacy between them. To support his proposal Kaunitz pointed out how limited the value of the alliance with Britain had been. Britain had followed her own interests throughout the previous war, and had not hesitated to put pressure on Austria to make concessions to Prussia in 1742 and 1745 so that she would concentrate on fighting France, the only enemy Britain was interested in. On the other hand, France as well as Austria had been humiliated by Prussia's victory, and might consider favourably a joint attack on this upstart state which had treated its alliance with France with so much contempt. With such arguments, Kaunitz was despatched to Paris in 1749 as the Austrian ambassador.

When Kaunitz arrived at the French court at Versailles he found that foreign policy was nominally controlled by Louis XV. However, it did not take him long to realise that Louis found affairs of state boring. His chief interests were hunting and a succession of mistresses. His current mistress was the sophisticated and intelligent Madame de Pompadour. Deciding that Pompadour was the power behind the throne, Kaunitz used all his considerable charm to try to persuade both her and the king that Austria was willing to forget old quarrels, and to promote the possibility of an alliance against Prussia.

Kaunitz stayed in France until 1753 when he was recalled to Vienna to become Foreign Minister. There is no doubt that he was a highly skilled diplomat who showed more originality than his rival, Frederick. Nevertheless, it is possible to overrate his achievements at this stage. When he left Versailles, relations between Austria and France were much friendlier than they had been for many years, but Louis had neither abandoned his good relations with Prussia, nor had he signed any alliance with Austria. Why did Louis not accept an Austrian alliance? It was not because he had made a cool assessment of the European situation, and decided he should concentrate all his resources on fighting Britain, avoiding all continental entanglements. Such a clear-headed realisation of France's limited resources and priorities were far beyond this amiable but lazy monarch. Rather, it was simply his indecisiveness that led him to refuse to commit French resources to a war against Prussia. It may also be that Kaunitz (like many other people) overrated Pompadour's influence over French policies and spent too much time cultivating her rather than Louis himself. When Kaunitz returned home, therefore, Austria was still a long way from creating an alliance strong enough to ensure the defeat of Prussia. Fortunately, Frederick's policies were now to come to Maria Theresa's aid.

c) Frederick's Policies

Frederick had an efficient spy network and was well aware of Kaunitz's attempts to gain the friendship of France. The prospect of the two strongest powers in Europe uniting for the sole purpose of crushing him was an alarming one, but Frederick was confident that, with their long history of distrust and emnity, there was no real prospect of such an alliance becoming reality. In his *Political Testament* of 1752 he summed up Prussia's current position.

1 By our geographical position, we are neighbours with the mightiest princes of Europe. Of all the powers of Europe, Austria is the one we have most offended, never willing to forget the loss of

Silesia or her authority in Germany, which we now share with
5 her. Prussia will never lack allies, particularly France. My present
intention is therefore to preserve peace. There could never be
another attack, like the one of Silesia, for imitation of a master-
piece invariably falls flat.

Frederick's confidence that France would stay friendly and that
Austria would never dare attack her whilst he possessed such a
powerful ally started to crumble in 1755. It is ironic that it was a quite
separate event which caused Frederick radically to change his policies.
In that year Britain had signed an alliance with Russia. The alliance
only lasted a few months, but it was enough to worry Frederick
seriously.

Empress Elizabeth of Russia had already made a treaty of friendship
with Maria Theresa. There was now the distinct possibility of Austria,
Russia and Britain forming an alliance against Prussia and France.
Frederick had not helped matters by his offensive remarks about
Elizabeth. He had commented that 'Elizabeth, Maria Theresa and
Madame de Pompadour are the three first whores of Europe'. His
dislike of female rulers, expressed in such a crude way, helped to ensure
that Elizabeth would become one of his deadliest enemies.

Frederick knew that fighting had already broken out in 1755 between
the British and French in America. It could only be a matter of time
before the two countries were formally at war. Frederick understood
that Britain was anxious to protect Hanover, her possession in Germany, from French attack when war was eventually declared. That was
the main reason for her proposed alliance with Russia. Prussia needed
to break the ring of states aligned against him, and accordingly offered a
treaty of friendship with Britain. In return for Britain abandoning her
friendship with Russia, Frederick undertook to protect Hanover.

The agreement was acceptable to Britain. After all, Prussia, the
neighbouring state, was far more capable of defending Hanover from
France than was Russia. In January 1756 the Convention of Westminster was signed. Frederick was well pleased with this treaty. He had split
a potentially dangerous coalition against him and thereby prevented a
war. In fact the treaty was a blunder. Far from ensuring the mainte-
nance of peace, it helped create the very coalition he most feared.

d) The Switch of Alliances

Frederick had initiated the first stage in the reversal of alliances which
is often, although perhaps misleadingly, termed 'the Diplomatic Revolution'. The term is misleading because it implies a more rapid and
unexpected change in the alliance system than was actually the case.
However, it is true that the Convention of Westminster persuaded
Louis XV to do something that all of Kaunitz's diplomacy had failed to

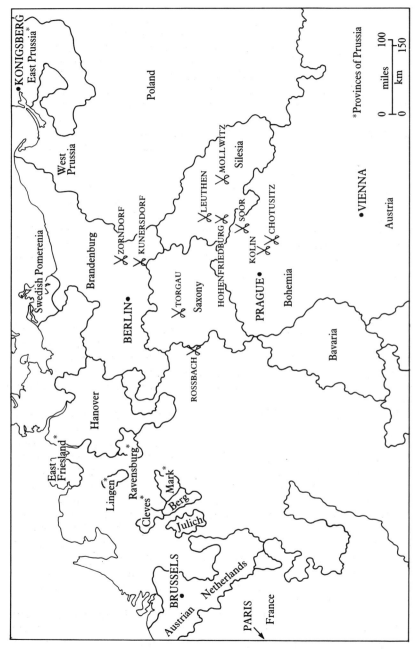

The Wars of Frederick the Great

achieve: in May 1756 he signed a Treaty of Friendship with Austria. This became known as the First Treaty of Versailles.

Louis had little choice but to improve relations with Austria. War was about to break out with Britain, and Prussia was Britain's ally. It was logical to come to terms with Prussia's main rival. In fact, the terms were purely defensive. France and Austria agreed not to fight each other and to protect each other's lands if they were attacked. It should be noted that the one thing Louis refused to do was to help Austria if she attacked Prussia. France would only help Austria if Prussia attacked first. But, as we have seen, Frederick had no wish to start another war.

The First Treaty of Versailles was a success for Louis XV, achieved more by luck than by any skill on his part. He had ensured a free hand for his war against Britain, which broke out in May 1756, without committing himself to any fighting in Europe. To Kaunitz's frustration, he found he had only gained France's friendship and neutrality, when what he needed was a French promise of help against Prussia. Kaunitz predicted it would be at least another year before he had enough allies to consider attacking Prussia.

e) The Prussian Conquest of Saxony

Once again it was Frederick who came to Austria's rescue. The treaty of friendship between France and Austria had been a complete surprise to him. He was now faced with the possibility of three of the great powers of Europe – Austria, France and Russia – combining against him. He was also aware that Kaunitz was actively working to bring other states into the alliance.

It was not in Frederick's nature to wait to be attacked. The events of 1740–8 had shown that he preferred to strike before his enemies were ready. Accordingly, when his spies reported in August 1756 that Prussia's neighbour Saxony was about to join the alliance against him, he did not hesitate. A glance at the map will show how dangerous it would have been to allow Saxony to attack him. It was, in fact, the only state among his enemies capable of striking easily at his homeland. He resolved to attack Saxony at once – a classic pre-emptive strike intended, not to annex the state, but to break up the coalition against him before it was ready. In August 1756 his armies attacked, and the Prussian *Blitzkrieg* again proved its effectiveness. The Saxons, caught totally by surprise, fought back well, but by the end of the year the state had been overrun. It appeared to be another dramatic success for Frederick. But was it?

Actually, the attack was a disastrous blunder. Saxony had not been about to ally with Austria – a good example of the dangers of rulers believing what their spies tell them. Frederick did not realise the impact his aggression would have on Europe. Even if Saxony *had* been planning to join his enemies, it is doubtful whether his conquest would have justified the consequences. As it was, Frederick acted rashly on the basis of misleading rumours because these confirmed his own mistaken belief that Kaunitz was weaving a web of alliances against him. In the event, it was Frederick, not Kaunitz, who created the anti-Prussian alliance.

Frederick tried to justify his attack on Saxony in a statement to the courts of Europe.

> 1 It is true that the King started hostilities, but this was not aggression. By aggression one means an action opposed to a peace treaty. An offensive league, incitement to war, planning the invasion of another prince – these things are aggression. He who
> 5 anticipates aggression may commit hostilities, but he is not the aggressor.

Frederick probably wrote these words truthfully. He honestly had no intention of annexing Saxony (although he did not hesitate to plunder its resources and recruit its men into his army), and he genuinely intended it as a purely defensive move to break up the coalition against him. That was not the way Europe saw it. A triumphant Kaunitz could now proclaim that *yet again* Prussia was attacking a helpless victim. He argued that Prussia was a state not to be trusted – one which represented a constant threat to its neighbours and to the peace of Europe – and that it was, in short, a country that needed to be cut down to size.

6 The Alliance against Prussia

The alliance against Prussia was not created overnight. For a few more months it was still possible to maintain that there were two quite separate wars taking place – that of Britain against France in the colonies and that of Austria and a conquered Saxony against Prussia in Germany. However, within a few months the combination of Kaunitz's diplomatic skills and the fear created by Frederick's attack on Saxony induced one country after another to join in a coalition against Prussia.

The first to join Austria was the Empire itself. In January 1757 the Imperial Diet denounced Frederick's aggression and mobilised its armed forces. Such an army, from past experience, was likely to be of poor quality, but the vote demonstrated how Austria had won the moral argument inside the Empire. It had been many years since the Diet had voted to support Austria against a fellow member of the Empire. Within a few weeks more substantial support came from Russia. In February 1757 Empress Elizabeth agreed to supply 80,000 men for the war. At this stage Russia asked nothing for herself in return for her help, but by a later agreement she was promised the province of East

Prussia. Russia was followed a month later by Sweden, which hoped to recover Eastern Pomerenia. However, the most important alliance remained to be secured. France remained reluctant to become involved in the war against Prussia. Louis XV wished to concentrate his resources on the war against Britain, and was at this time on bad terms with Russia. On the other hand, Prussia had clearly conducted an act of aggression; Prussia was the ally of France's enemy Britain; and Louis still deluded himself that he had the power and resources to fight two wars at once. There was also a personal factor. Louis XV's son had married the daughter of the Elector of Saxony. Louis, who had previously fought a war (the Polish Succession, 1733–8) on behalf of his father-in-law, now found it difficult to refuse to help his daughter-in-law's family.

The Second Treaty of Versailles (May 1757) was a very different document from the first treaty, signed exactly a year previously. France now agreed to supply 100,000 men and to pay Austria 12 million florins a year. Prussia was to be dismembered, with Silesia going to Austria, Magdeburg to a revived Saxony and East Pomerenia to Sweden. Prussia was also to lose Cleves and the small province of Gelderland.

The effect of this treaty, alongside the one promising East Prussia to Russia, would have been to remove nearly all the lands Prussia had so painstakingly acquired over the previous century. Prussia would be reduced to Brandenburg alone, and would revert to being just another unimportant small state of the Empire. The main beneficiary of the proposed partition would have been Austria. Maria Theresa would have regained both her land and her undisputed primacy within the Empire.

What is less clear is what France stood to gain from the treaty. In return for a commitment of a large sum of money and a sizeable army for an indefinite time, France was promised as her reward just three towns (Ostend, Nieuport and Ypres) in the Austrian Netherlands. It is a measure of Louis' weakness that he agreed to offer so much help to Austria when *even if Austria won* he stood to get so little in return. It is also a measure of Kaunitz's skill that he was able to use the attack on Saxony to such good effect to turn the First Treaty, in which France offered very little of substance, into the Second Treaty in which France offered so much.

Kaunitz had triumphed, helped not a little by Frederick's mistakes and Louis' weakness. The allies outnumbered Prussia in every respect – in terms of population, for example, by more than twenty to one. Frederick's only ally, Britain, was solely interested in colonies and the protection of Hanover. Prussia, in practice, would have to fight alone in Europe. There was now little doubt in Maria Theresa's mind that Frederick was doomed.

7 The First Year of the War

Frederick was never a man to wait for his enemies to gather their armies. Having knocked out one enemy, Saxony, in 1756, he resolved to defeat his most determined opponent, Austria, before the other allies could reach him. When the campaigning season opened in May 1757 he invaded Bohemia, quickly won one battle and captured Prague. Events then went badly wrong. The Prussian army was defeated at the Battle of Kolin by the able but cautious Austrian general, Daun. This was, in fact, the first time the Prussian army had lost a battle since Frederick's wars had begun in 1740. But Kolin did more than break the myth of Prussian invincibility and encourage the Austrians. It forced Frederick to abandon Bohemia and to retreat back into Silesia.

His enemies were now able to close in. A French army attacked Hanover, the Russians attacked East Prussia and the Swedes moved into Pomerenia. A second French army commanded by Soubise, a favourite of Madame de Pompadour, linked up with Imperial army and together marched on Prussia. Finally an Austrian army reconquered most of Silesia. It seemed as if the war would all be over before the end of the year.

Frederick now achieved the most remarkable triumph of his career. Abandoning Silesia and East Prussia to the enemy for the moment, he quickly marched his army to face the huge Franco-Imperial army at the Battle of Rossbach (November 1757). Although outnumbered by two to one, he won a crushing victory. In just three hours the Prussians killed or captured some 16,000 soldiers for the loss of just 500 of their own men. Although the figures give some indications of how total and rapid Frederick's victory was, they do not explain its impact. At a stroke Prussia had virtually knocked both France and the Imperial army out of the war. The battle encouraged Britain to start providing Frederick with military and financial support since Frederick was being so effective at weakening the French. The victory at Rossbach made Prussia's western border safe, allowing Frederick to concentrate on fighting Austria and Russia. Yet even these effects are less important than the long-term implications of this first ever defeat of France at the hands of a Prussian army. On 5 November 1757 French military supremacy in Europe, which had lasted for some 130 years, came to an end.

Why did Frederick win this battle so easily? He faced a second rate army, comprised of reluctant Imperial troops mixed uneasily with French soldiers – a good example of the dangers of multi-national armies fighting a determined foe. The commander, Soubise, was inexperienced and over-confident. Worse still, his army was short of supplies because another general refused to send the necessary equipment after a quarrel. Soubise himself owed his appointment to his friendship with Pompadour. Louis' willingness to appoint a commander on the personal recommendation of his mistress is an indication of the way in which he ran the affairs of state.

Frederick did not relax after Rossbach. He moved his army, at the speed of which only the Prussians were capable, to fight the Austrians in Silesia. Exactly one month after Rossbach he routed the Austrian army at Leuthen and drove them out of Silesia. Leuthen was a very different affair to Rossbach. Here Frederick was fighting no playboy general with a divided army. This time he faced a battle-tested army commanded by the same generals who had beaten him at Kolin. This makes his achievement all the more remarkable. The Prussian army killed or captured some 49,000 Austrians for the loss of 12,000 of its own men. The figures indicate that this was both a bloodier battle and a harder fight than Rossbach. Nevertheless, Frederick's victory was just as complete. Here he owed his victory to his generalship and his men. He conducted an 'oblique attack'. He launched a feint attack to pin down the Austrians, then split his army and marched half of it round to attack the enemy in the flank. They were unable to react in time and the flank was rolled up. Only an army as well-drilled as the Prussians could march so rapidly and in such good order round to the flank of the enemy. Only a general as skilled and confident as Frederick would have divided his smaller army in the face of the enemy after the battle had already started.

These two battles established Frederick's reputation as a master of the battlefield. He was hailed as 'the Protestant Hero' – a somewhat ironic title, in view of his own lack of religious principles – and he even had inns named after him in Britain. Now nobody begrudged him the title of 'the Great'. He had destroyed the armies of two of his most dangerous enemies in just four weeks. He had ensured that his name would reach the history books as he hoped – these two battles are still studied at military academies today. Frederick clearly hoped that these victories would induce France and Austria to admit defeat and end the war.

8 The Campaign of 1758

Frederick's hopes were to be disappointed. When the campaigning season opened in 1758, it was clear that all his enemies were still very much in the war against him. However, his two victories did lead to one major improvement in his situation. The new British Prime Minister, William Pitt the Elder, agreed to offer Frederick much more assistance. This came in two forms. There was an annual cash subsidy of around £650,000, which was to prove vital in the years to come. There was also a sizeable army stationed in Hanover under the command of the capable Prince Ferdinand of Brunswick. This army protected Prussia's western flank and in particular ensured that Frederick would never again be threatened by a French army.

However, Prussia still had to face the Austrians and the Russians alone. At first the events of 1757 repeated themselves. Frederick struck first, invading Moravia in April 1758. The Austrians cut his supply lines and forced him back to Silesia. The Russian army had conquered East Prussia and then crossed Poland to attack Brandenburg itself. In August 1758 Frederick found himself in a battle with a Russian army for the first time in his life. Once again, at the Battle of Zorndorf, Frederick won the day, but this was no repeat of the easy victories of 1757. The Russians were driven out of Brandenburg, but retained East Prussia. Frederick lost 13,000 men – nearly as many as the Russians – and was astonished at how fiercely the Russian soldiers fought, even when surrounded and in a hopeless position.

The Austrians took advantage of Frederick's absence to invade Saxony and Silesia. Frederick quickly returned to fight the Austrians but was defeated by Daun at Hochkirch (October 1758). Fortunately for the Prussians, Daun, cautious as ever, failed to follow up his victory. Frederick now showed that it was not always necessary to fight battles in order to win campaigns. By rapid movements he cut Daun off from his supply lines. With winter approaching, Daun abandoned his conquests in Saxony and Silesia and retired to his bases in Bohemia.

Once again Frederick ended the year still in control of all his lands (except East Prussia) and of Saxony as well. But his situation was in every other respect worse than it had been in 1757. His enemies were learning from their mistakes and were fighting much more effectively, while his own army was suffering from irreplaceable losses of men, particularly officers. By 1759 the brilliant fighting machine which had been built up so carefully by his father and which had performed so well since 1740 was being seriously weakened. Only Frederick's own skill remained unchanged.

9 The Campaign of 1759

In the west, France, now approaching exhaustion and bankruptcy and suffering heavy defeats at the hands of the British in the colonies, made one last effort to intervene in Germany. But so effective was British help that the attempt did not distract Frederick at all. Prince Ferdinand's Hanoverian army routed the French at Minden (August 1759). Although France stayed nominally in the war until the end, her armies never again tried to intervene against Prussia. It is ironic that Kaunitz had gone to so much trouble to gain an alliance with France when that alliance proved to be of so little value to Austria.

Despite the good news from Hanover, this should have been the year in which Frederick lost the war. His two most formidable enemies, Austria and Russia, at last agreed to combine their armies to crush him. Frederick was unable to prevent the two armies uniting and he had to fight a combined force considerably larger than his own at Kunersdorf

(August 1759). The result was a total defeat for Frederick, as catastrophic in its way as Rossbach or Leuthen. It was not only the loss of men – about 19,000 were killed or captured – but that the survivors were scattered in all directions. The next day Frederick found his army reduced to just 3,000 men. He had no way of replacing his army and there was now nothing to stop his enemies from overrunning all his provinces. The war was over and Frederick, after winning amazing victories against heavy odds, had finally succumbed to superior numbers. It is no surprise that in his despair he contemplated suicide as he wrote to his Foreign Minister:

1 My coat is riddled with musket balls and I had two horses killed under me. It is my misfortune that I am still alive. Our losses are very great, and I only have 3,000 out of 48,000 men left. At the moment everyone is in flight and I have no control over my men.
5 You should now think of your own safety. I shall not survive this cruel turn of fortune. The consequences will be worse than the defeat itself. I have no resources left. I believe everything is lost. I shall not outlive the downfall of my country. Farewell forever!

Yet Frederick survived to fight another day. General Daun took advantage of the Prussian collapse to recapture most of Saxony, but the Russians, instead of overrunning Brandenburg, returned to their bases in East Prussia. These unexpected developments enabled Frederick to rebuild his army and even to retain Silesia. The failure of the allies to complete the destruction of Prussia on the one occasion they had the opportunity to do so remains one of the most remarkable occurrences of this war.

There were a number of reasons for this blunder. The Russians felt (perhaps rightly) that the Austrians had not fought as hard as they could have done at Kunersdorf. The Russian commander, Saltykov, quarrelled with Daun over this and then withdrew his troops in disgust. After all, Russia had already achieved its objective in the war (East Prussia), so there was no need to help their ungrateful ally further. Another factor was the known ill-health of Empress Elizabeth. She was a determined enemy of Frederick, but her nephew and heir, Peter, was known to admire Frederick. Once he became tsar, he would probably make peace with Prussia. It would not do Saltykov's career any good to be fighting the Prussians when Peter ascended the throne.

However, these factors cannot completely explain the reluctance of the allies to follow up their victory. They were aware that they had defeated Frederick, but not of the disintegration of his army after the battle. As far as they knew, Frederick still commanded a formidable force. They moved slowly because they expected him to spring a surprise on them as he had so often in the past. It was here that Frederick's reputation, based on his previous victories, came to his rescue. Daun and Saltykov were haunted by the memories of Leuthen and Zorndorf, and did not want to throw away their advantage by being too hasty.

There was one further factor in Frederick's survival. This was the loyalty of his own subjects. In his hour of need, his people, from whom he had never asked for or expected devotion, rallied to his cause. There was an outpouring of patriotism, and many men volunteered to replace the soldiers who had died at Kunersdorf. No doubt much of this was simply due to fear of the enemy – the pillaging of the Russian army was notorious – but again, a pride in their king's achievements and a recognition of his determination may also have made possible his survival. Both at home and abroad the reputation of Frederick 'the Great' came to his aid in his hour of need. Frederick deserved both that reputation and the stroke of luck that it brought him in 1759.

10 The Campaigns of 1760–2

Frederick was able to rebuild his army to a strength of 100,000 men by the time the campaigning season opened in 1760. However, the decline in its quality was noticeable. It has been estimated that 80 per cent of the officers of 1756 were now dead, and in his desperation he was recruiting officers who were aged only 13. The Austrians and Russians were also showing signs of exhaustion, and neither side fought with as much determination as they had in the past. Increasingly the war degenerated into one of manoeuvre, as each side tried to cut off the supply routes of the other while preferring not to risk their increasingly precious soldiers in battle.

1760 was the last year in which Frederick demonstrated his genius in battle. He defeated the Austrians at Liegnitz in August and followed this up with a victory in November at Torgau where he again demonstrated his mastery of the battlefield. These victories enabled Prussia to retain Silesia and to recover half of Saxony, although the Austrians still held on to Dresden, the capital, which they had captured in the aftermath of Kunersdorf. By contrast, in 1761 there were no significant battles at all. It seemed that Frederick was going to retain all his conquests as his enemies were clearly unable to make the final effort that was required to destroy him. Although his army was exhausted, he was aware that for their part the Austrians were facing bankruptcy, and that their armies were desperately short of supplies.

It was at this moment that a disaster occurred comparable to that of Kunersdorf. So long as William Pitt remained Prime Minister, British gold flowed into Prussia's coffers. However, in 1761 Pitt's government fell and Bute, the new Prime Minister, saw no reason to continue with the subsidies. After all, the British were paying the Prussians to fight the French, but Frederick had not faced them in battle since 1757. Without warning, the subsidies were ended. Unable to finance his army, Frederick faced total collapse in 1762. The Austrians would now be able to recapture Silesia without a fight. Frederick was naturally very bitter about this British betrayal, although it could be argued that Britain was only adopting the cynical use of allies which Frederick had himself pioneered in the War of Austrian Succession.

With disaster looming, there now came what Frederick himself described as 'the miracle of the house of Brandenburg'. In January 1762 Empress Elizabeth of Russia died after a long illness. She was succeeded by her nephew, Peter III, a tsar of considerable eccentricity whose favourite pastime was playing with his huge army of model soldiers. Peter greatly admired Frederick, and had made it clear that as soon as he became tsar he would end the war with Prussia. He was as good as his word. The Russian army was at once ordered to cease operations and within a short time a peace treaty was signed. Not only did Russia drop out of the war, but Peter returned East Prussia to Frederick. This was the province that Russian armies had captured in 1758 and which Frederick had thought was permanently lost. Peter now went even further, offering to become Prussia's ally and to fight the Austrians. In fact Frederick was never able to take up this offer. Within a short time, Peter was overthrown in a military *coup d'état*, murdered and replaced by his wife, who ruled as Catherine II. She decided not to assist Frederick in his wars, but equally rejected suggestions that she might renew the alliance with Austria.

It is usual for historians to agree with Frederick that Peter III's change of sides was a stroke of astonishing good fortune for Prussia which could not have come at a better time. In an age when the personality of the monarch was often crucial, the fact that a young tsar happened to hero-worship a Prussian king explains this reversal of Russian policy. At a stroke all the gains made by the Russians in six years of war were abandoned by an apparently mad tsar. But this explanation does not do justice to Peter's motives. Peter admired Frederick for a reason. Frederick had been a living legend throughout Peter's life. Peter, who could only command armies of toy soldiers, longed to be a real hero like Frederick. Once again, as in the events following Kunersdorf, it was Frederick's own reputation which helped save him at a moment of crisis.

11 The End of the War

a) The Treaty of Hubertusburg

In early 1763 it became clear that the war must end soon. Russia had already signed a peace treaty with Prussia. The news that Britain and France had signed a peace treaty (the Treaty of Paris) in February 1763 meant that only Austria and Prussia were now still fighting. Maria Theresa and Kaunitz reluctantly accepted that the coalition had come to an end and that Austria would be unable to defeat Prussia on her own. Within a week of the Treaty of Paris, Austria and Prussia signed the Treaty of Hubertusburg. Prussia could keep Silesia. In return Saxony would be returned to its elector, and Frederick would vote for Maria Theresa's son as the next Holy Roman Emperor. In short, the Seven Years War did not change the European borders of any of the states that took part in it. Nevertheless, it had been one of the most important wars of the eighteenth century.

b) The Effects of the War

Although no land changed hands by the Treaty of Hubertusburg, the war had important effects on all the states that were involved in it. Of these states, Great Britain was the most successful. The war saw her emerge as one of the strongest powers in Europe. While Austria and Prussia had fought each other to exhaustion on the continent, Britain had enjoyed a series of successful campaigns in the colonies. Helped by control of the seas, some able commanders, and the clear aims and leadership of William Pitt, her forces had overrun much of the French colonial empire. At the Treaty of Paris, the British annexation of the French colonies in North America and India was confirmed. Just as important was the acquisition of a number of small but economically valuable sugar-producing islands in the the West Indies. Britain had certainly been helped by the fact that French resources were being diverted into the war against Frederick. However, it is likely that even without Frederick's help, Britain would have defeated the French in this war, although it is unlikely that they would have enjoyed quite such spectacular success.

Russia also emerged from the war with credit, although with no gains in territory. The Russian army had fought extremely well – it had been the only one which had demonstrated the ability both to defeat the Prussian army (at Kunersdorf) and to conquer and hold Prussian territory (East Prussia). Although Peter III's strange behaviour ensured that Russia did not keep her conquests, the fact that Russian forces were operating successfully in central Europe was a portent for the future. Under Catherine the Great (1762–96) Russia was to fulfil the potential it had first shown during Elizabeth's reign. By 1763 Russia and Britain were probably the two strongest powers in Europe.

While states on the fringes of continental Europe were using the war to help increase their strength, the great powers on mainland Europe found theirs in decline. Of these, the most surprising was Prussia itself. Certainly in many ways Prussia emerged from the war with credit. Frederick had successfully beaten off a formidable coalition virtually single-handed and ensured Prussia's retention of Silesia. It was now beyond dispute that Prussia was one of the Great Powers of Europe, and that Frederick was a ruler of the highest quality. His military skill had been second to none, and he clearly deserved his title of 'the Great'. Other than his contemporary Catherine, who also received (with far less justification) the same flattering epithet, he was to be the last ruler in European history to receive this title.

Yet for all the undoubted achievements of both Prussia in general and Frederick in particular during the war, it is very doubtful whether the state emerged stronger as a result of it. Prussia was exhausted and bankrupt. It has been estimated that its population fell by 500,000 between 1756 and 1763. Some 60,000 horses and 13,000 houses were destroyed, and Frederick estimated the total cost of the war at 140 million thalers – the equivalent of 20 years income from taxes. It would take Prussia many years to recover from the ravages of the fighting. Certainly Silesia was a valuable acquisition, but the cost of its conquest in human and financial terms had been enormous. Its retention had clearly established Frederick's prestige and greatness, but it is open to question whether Prussia would have been better off in terms of cost if Frederick had never attacked the province. Frederick himself never doubted that he had been right to seize Silesia and felt that the heavy price Prussia paid for it was justified. But he could not know whether his long-suffering people would have agreed with him – and nor would he have cared.

Austria was undoubtedly weakened by the war. Despite all the advantages of having numerous allies, Maria Theresa had failed to recapture her lost province. This was a clear indication that Austrian supremacy over Germany was at an end. From now on, she would have to share her power with Prussia. Austria had become as exhausted as Prussia by the long war. By 1762 Maria Theresa was forced to reduce the size of the army and to print ever larger quantities of paper money as her ability to pay for the war came to an end. It is possible that Austrian participation in the war served as a reminder to Europe in general and Prussia in particular that Austria remained a power to be reckoned with, and that her days of weakness of 1740–2 were definitely at an end, but these were small consolations for Maria Theresa's definite failure, despite enjoying several advantages, to regain Silesia.

The state which was most heavily defeated in the war was France. Louis XV ended the war with most of his colonial empire seized by Britain and facing total bankruptcy. His prestige in Europe had been destroyed by the contemptuous ease with with his armies had been defeated at Rossbach and Minden. He was himself despised by his own people, who were to greet his death in 1774 with delight. It had been some centuries since a French monarch had been so comprehensively humiliated as Louis XV was in 1763, and the defeat was made all the worse because previously Louis had deluded himself that France remained the strongest state in Europe. The fact that France lost no land in Europe was no real consolation. Even the retention of the alliance with Austria after 1763 probably did more harm than good. To set the seal on the renewed alliance, the *Dauphin* Louis (later Louis XVI) was married to Marie-Antoinette, the daughter of Maria Theresa. This was to prove to be an ill-fated and tragic royal marriage. From the start, Marie-Antoinette was disliked by the people of France, and the sneering nickname they gave her, *L'Autrichienne* (the Austrian), was a constant reminder of how much they blamed their monarch's alliance with Austria for their troubles. The combination of military defeat, loss of land, bankruptcy, loss of prestige, the loss of personal popularity and a disastrously unpopular marriage all helped lay the seeds for the Revolution of 1789.

However, the war did have one beneficial effect on France, although few realised it at the time. After the disaster of Rossbach, the French army was at last obliged to modernise itself. In the years that followed, new training, drill and weapons were introduced. By the 1780s the French army had recovered its effectiveness. It was in this modernised army that young officers like Napoleon Bonaparte were to learn their craft. It is doubtful whether the French army would have undertaken such a transformation without the shock of defeat.

c) Why did Prussia Survive?

By any standards, Prussia's survival during the Seven Years War was a remarkable achievement. Heavily outnumbered from the start, facing the armies of three great powers, any one of which enjoyed far greater resources than he could hope to command, Frederick the Great emerged in 1763 with his territories intact, his prestige at its highest, and his enemies humiliated. A number of factors had enabled this to happen.

The first of these was unity of command. Frederick was now unique in that he was the last of the soldier-kings, that generation of monarchs who led their troops in person. Other monarchs – Elizabeth, Maria Theresa, Louis XV and even George II – now left such matters in the hands of professional generals. In Frederick's hands, however, the combination of being head of state and effective head of the army gave Prussia united command and decisive leadership which the other countries very obviously lacked. The unity of command and the efficient management of the resources of his state were the result of the work of his father, and Frederick William must take some of the credit for Prussia's survival. For it was he who provided and trained the army and who created the efficient administrative and financial systems which survived the test of war so much better than their French or Austrian counterparts.

Frederick's own ability as a commander must also rank highly as a factor. He was an original strategist, who developed the idea of the 'oblique attack', but in addition he was an inspiration to his troops. He led his men in person and showed considerable bravery during a number of battles. There was no trace now of the hesitantcy which he had shown during his first battle at Mollwitz. Above all, he showed complete determination, never fearing heavy odds and quickly recovering from the worst defeats. His despair after Kunersdorf was understandable: more impressive was his rapid recovery from it. Eventually his success became infectious. It inspired his troops to enormous efforts and caused his enemies either to fear him (as Daun demonstrated after Kunersdorf) or, as in the case of Peter III, to admire him. Frederick was one of the great captains of war, one of the three finest generals of the eighteenth century (the others being Marlborough and Napoleon), and amongst the best in the whole history of Europe. It would be difficult to overstate his personal contribution to Prussia's survival.

Prussia enjoyed some advantages of geography. Its core (Brandenburg) was still relatively small and compact, and Frederick could take advantage of interior lines of communication to move quickly from one threatened sector to another within it. By contrast, the allies all had to move long distances even to reach the borders of Prussia. As a result, a combined attack on Prussia was very difficult to co-ordinate.

The disunity of Frederick's enemies was another major factor. Only once, in 1759, did they effectively combine their armies. It was typical of the lack of common purpose amongst the allies that the two victorious generals quarrelled as soon as the battle was over and went their separate ways, so enabling Frederick to survive. This disunity was itself a result of the differing aims of the allies. The failure of the allies to combine their armies was one example of the mistakes made by them. There were many others, including Maria Theresa's reliance on generals who were her relations rather than those who were competent, and Louis XV's appointment of Soubise. Some historians would consider it reasonable to argue that the allies lost the war through their mistakes and lack of unity, rather than that Frederick won it through skill and determination.

The contribution of Britain to Frederick's survival was also significant. She distracted the French and ensured the safety of Prussia's western borders, enabling Frederick to concentrate solely on fighting Austria and Russia after 1757. The value of her subsidies to Frederick is clearly demonstrated by the immediate collapse of his financial system when they were withdrawn in 1761. Finally, the loyalty of the Prussian people, particularly in Frederick's hour of need in 1759, was also a significant factor.

Finally we cannot ignore the part played by luck. Napoleon later said that this was the most important quality a successful general needed, and it must be admitted that Frederick was often lucky. He was fortunate in never having to face combined armies for long, that he so often fought cautious or incompetent generals, and that his two most formidable enemies quarrelled instead of destroying him in 1759. Above all, he was fortunate that Elizabeth died when she did and that

Peter III admired him so much. But although Frederick certainly enjoyed his share of good fortune, what marked him out as a great general was that he knew how to take advantage of it.

Frederick's attack on Silesia led to two terrible wars which dominated European affairs for 23 years. Prussia emerged at the end as one of the great powers of Europe. It is difficult not to feel some repugnance at the way Frederick attacked weak countries and at the lack of any moral or legal claim to Silesia. Equally, it is difficult not to feel admiration for the skill and determination he showed in holding on to his spoils.

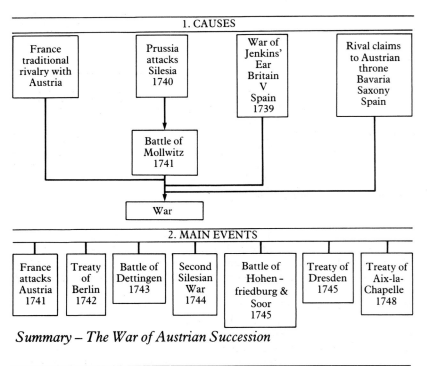

Summary – The War of Austrian Succession

Making notes on 'Habsburgs versus Hohenzollerns'

When reading this chapter, it is easy to get bogged down in details of diplomatic history or to be alarmed at an apparently endless list of campaigns and battles whose names and dates you think you are expected to remember. It should help you to make realistic notes if you bear in mind that you will never be expected, in an examination, to give a detailed account of the diplomacy of the period. Nor will you be expected to know the technicalities of weapons and military tactics of the time.

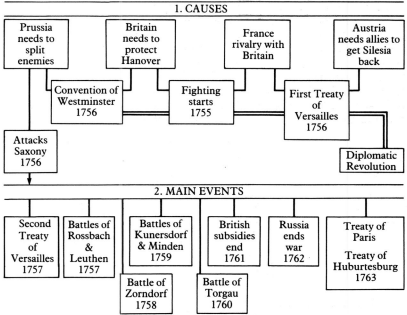

Summary – The Seven Years War

The main issues you do need to be confident about are:
i)   The reasons why Frederick II decided to attack Silesia in 1740
ii)   How and why this attack led to a general war in Europe in 1741
iii) How and why Prussia emerged as the only winner in the War of Austrian Succession
iv)   How and why Austria formed an alliance with France
v)   How and why war came to Europe in 1756
vi)   Why Prussia was able to survive the Seven Years War
vii) The effects of the Seven Years War.

Make your notes under these seven headings. In each case make *explanations* the core of what you write. Only include facts to illustrate the general points that you make.

Answering essay questions on 'Habsburgs versus Hohenzollerns'

Questions on Frederick II's wars are frequently asked in examinations. Sometimes the question demands a comparison between Frederick's achievements in wartime and in peacetime; such questions will be looked at in chapter 6. But you will often find questions based solely on his foreign policy and its impact on Europe, and it is these questions we will look at now.

Consider the following questions:

1 Why did Frederick the Great involve Prussia in a European war in 1740?

2 Why did the conflict between Prussia and Austria over Silesia last so long?

3 Why was Prussia able to survive the Seven Years War?

4 What were the immediate and long-term consequences of Frederick's invasion of Silesia?

5 What were the consequences of the Diplomatic Revolution?

6 In what ways did the Seven Years War alter the European balance of power?

7 Consider the view that the military victories of Frederick the Great were the decisive stage in Prussia's rise to great-power status.

8 Trace the growth of Prussia as a European power between 1713 and 1763.

9 'It was the Seven Years War which made Prussia a Great Power'. Discuss.

You will notice that the essays have been arranged into three groups. What do questions 1 to 3 have in common? The answer is to be found in the first word of each one. Such questions require the creation of a list of factors or causes – each one normally beginning with the word 'because'. It does not matter greatly in which order these factors are described in your answer, but your conclusion must discuss which of the factors or causes dealt with were the more important. Of course, you may decide that all the causes were of equal importance – but you must still explain this in your conclusion. You should particularly note that in questions like these, it is not necessary to go through the factors or causes in chronological order. On the contrary, a chronological approach may well lead you into writing an essay dominated by narrative, rather than one based on analysis. This is one of the most common causes of candidates doing less well than they had expected in examinations. You would normally wish to identify at least five or six major factors in any such essay. If there are other, less important causes, describe them together briefly in a single paragraph.

Produce an essay plan for question 3. Start by listing the five or six main reasons why Frederick survived. Which other reasons would you judge to be less important but worth a mention? Are there one or two factors in Frederick's survival which are more important than the others? Would you discuss these first?

Questions 4 to 6 ask you to discuss consequences. Here too the approach would be to describe the five or six most important effects of the event specified in the essay title, to offer supporting evidence for each one, and to be prepared to make some sort of judgement on which were the most important effects.

What is the unifying factor in questions 7 to 9? Here the common thread is provided by the subject matter rather than by the type of question. In order to be able to answer any of these questions, you need to have a clear idea of what the term Great Power means. Although it is not essential (but it is desirable) to include a definition in your essay, you do need to have a clear idea of what the term implies if you are going to be able to judge at what point Prussia reached that position.

Prepare a one-sentence definition of a Great Power. You are now in a position to establish how Prussia became a Great Power. This is one type of essay where a broadly chronological approach is justified. Do not make the mistake of thinking you are restricted to the reign of Frederick the Great. If your definition includes (as it should) the idea that a Great Power has a government, financial system and army capable of sustaining a successful war and conquering land, then you will also need to refer back to Frederick William's reign as providing the pre-conditions for Great Power status.

Question 8 offers a typical 'challenging statement' where the examiner puts forward his own suggestion for when Prussia became a Great Power. The examiner expects you to discuss in some depth the arguments for and against the Seven Years War marking the key moment, but that does *not* mean he either expects you to agree with the statement, or that the whole essay must be devoted to the Seven Years War. In fact, you would be unwise to agree too strongly with the statement, since it clearly oversimplifies the issues.

Make a list of the arguments *in favour* of the Seven Years War marking the moment Prussia became a Great Power (eg, ability to survive a war against three major powers). Make a list of the arguments for the idea that Prussia became a Great Power much earlier (eg, at the time of the conquest of Silesia, or of Frederick William's reforms).

Overall, when do you think Prussia could class itself as a Great Power?

Source based questions on 'Habsburgs versus Hohenzollerns'

1 Justifications for war
Carefully read the three extracts on pages 56 and 57. Answer the following questions.
a) Summarise the arguments Frederick uses in each of the three documents for going to war. (*6 marks*)
b) Each document was written with a different audience in mind. Who were the different documents written for? (*3 marks*)

c)   How reliable do you consider the documents to be in explaining Frederick's real reasons for going to war? *(4 marks)*
d)   To what extent do these sources support the view that 'Frederick II was the most immoral and dangerous ruler of his age'? *(7 marks)*

2 The Diplomatic Revolution and the Seven Years War

Carefully read the extracts on pages 66–7 and 75. Answer the following questions.

a)   Explain what Frederick meant by i) 'the mightiest princes of Europe' (page 66 lines 1–2), ii) and 'cruel turn of fortune' (page 75 line 6). *(3 marks)*
b)   How does Frederick explain his need for peace in the 1750s? *(3 marks)*
c)   Why did Frederick think Prussia 'will never lack allies' (page 67 line 5)? *(4 marks)*
d)   Discuss the validity of Frederick's claim that his attack on Saxony was not aggression. *(5 marks)*
e)   'If Frederick faced defeat and suicide in 1759 he only had himself to blame'. To what extent do these sources support this claim? *(5 marks)*

CHAPTER 5

Maria Theresa

1 Austria in 1740

When Maria Theresa ascended the throne of Austria in 1740 at the age of 23, she found her empire in a deplorable state. Her inheritance could hardly have been in sharper contrast to that of her contemporary, Frederick II of Prussia. While he inherited a large, well-trained army, a healthy financial situation and a strong centralised system of government, Maria Theresa found only problems.

The ministers she inherited from her father did not inspire confidence. They were, almost without exception, elderly and incompetent. Some of them were also corrupt. The Commander-in-Chief of the army was not only also in his seventies, but had been fortunate not to be court-martialled for his incompetence in the recent war against Turkey. He commanded an army low in numbers, equipment and morale. It is perhaps not surprising that when Frederick II attacked Austria (see chapter 4), these ministers advised Maria Theresa to 'negotiate' with Prussia rather than risk a war.

The finances were in a poor state. The Finance Minister informed Maria Theresa that less than 100,000 florins (or guilders) were available to her, taxes and loans for the coming months had already been spent, and that the national debt had increased enormously as a result of the war with Turkey. The Habsburg Empire was virtually bankrupt and in no position to consider expanding the army or fighting a war.

The attitude of the provinces was a cause for concern. Whilst it was true all of the provincial estates had accepted the Pragmatic Sanction without protest, even the more loyal Estates viewed the new monarch with some suspicion. It was widely believed that this young, inexperienced female ruler must inevitably have her policies dictated by her husband, Francis of Lorraine, who was not merely a foreigner but was also widely believed (quite unfairly) to be under the influence of France.

Charles VI's failure to tackle the weaknesses of his Empire had left Maria Theresa to face several long-standing problems, including the power and wealth of the Roman Catholic Church, the virtual independance of the Hungarian nobility, the backwardness of the economy and the existence of deep social, racial and religious divisions within society.

Finally there was Maria Theresa's own inexperience, of which she was painfully aware. She later wrote that 'I found myself without money, without credit, without an army, without experience or knowledge, even without advice, because all my ministers were wholly occupied in trying to guess which way the cat would jump'. She had never attended meetings of the Council of State before her accession, and only discovered the true state of the finances, army and administration once her father had died.

The new empress needed time to establish herself on her throne and to start to learn how to govern her divided empire. Frederick's invasion of Silesia deprived her of that opportunity. The War of Austrian Succession demonstrated that the Habsburg Empire could not continue as a great power without its system of administration being reformed. Maria Theresa later explained in a letter to her son, Joseph, how the war led her to consider reforms.

1 When I saw that the Peace of Dresden (1745) would have to be accepted, my way of thinking changed and turned exclusively to the internal condition of my territories, to the problem of protecting the Hereditary Lands against such powerful enemies
5 as Prussia and Turkey, when fortresses and money were lacking and our armies weak.

The role of the House of Habsburg had changed completely; it could no longer think of holding the balance against France, but only of its own preservation. After the Peace of Dresden it was my
10 sole endeavour to learn about the condition of my territories; then to conduct a thorough examination of the abuses which had crept into them, for it appeared that everything was in a state of the utmost confusion and chaos. It was not difficult to appreciate that, with the situation as it had existed hitherto, the monarchy
15 could not survive for long.

She then went on to identify the specific 'defects' which were weakening Austria. These were 'the form of government', officials working for themselves rather than 'serving me', too much red tape, and most serious of all, the power and independence enjoyed by the separate chancelleries. Her solution was, on paper at least, simple and dramatic.

1   After careful consideration, I decided that the decayed old system would have to be changed completely, at the centre and in the provinces, and that its replacement would be based firmly on the principles of systematic order. This would end the abuses and
5 disorder which had existed for such a long time.

Maria Theresa had neatly summarised some of the weaknesses of the Austrian state, and laid out for herself a clear programme of reform. She hoped to achieve for Austria what Frederick William had for Prussia. This chapter will consider whether or not she achieved these aims.

2 The Reform of Government

One of Maria Theresa's skills, which had been conspicuously lacking in her father, was her ability to choose able ministers to help her with her work. The reform of government in the early years of her reign was largely the responsibility of Count Friedrich Haugwitz. He was a Silesian nobleman who preferred to work in the Austrian service after Frederick II of Prussia conquered his lands in 1740. He had demonstrated a capacity for hard work, honesty and a commitment to efficient government when he was put in charge of administration first of the small rump of Silesia still controlled by Austria (1741–7) and then of Carinthia (1747–9). His administration was clearly modelled on the Prussian system of government, and he made no secret of his view that it was essential for Austria to copy Prussia if she was to survive as a Great Power. As early as 1743 he sent Maria Theresa a detailed plan for the reorganisation of local government throughout the Empire. In 1747 his plans for the reform of the tax system were adopted by the empress against the objections of the Council of State. From that time Haugwitz became Maria Theresa's indispensable partner in the reform programme.

a) Central Government

One of Haugwitz's aims was to copy Frederick's centralised system of government. A start was made in 1749 with the merging of the administrations of Austria and Bohemia under a committee which he chaired. This committee, the *Direktorium*, was clearly modelled on the Prussian General Directory both in its name and its proposed functions. There was bitter opposition to this strengthening of royal control, particularly from the Bohemian nobles and Diets which had enjoyed a measure of independence for centuries. Haugwitz was able to push through the change since the Bohemian diets had failed to oppose the French invasion of 1741; now they were being punished for their disloyalty. This extension of royal power to one of the largest provinces in the empire might have represented a significant shift to a centralised system of government.

The *Direktorium* proved to be too clumsy and unwieldy to handle a wide range of government business. Its control never extended to the new Chancelleries for Foreign Affairs (1742) and Justice (1748). It performed disappointingly during the Seven Years War (1756–63) and this, combined with the death of Haugwitz, allowed Maria Theresa's other main adviser, Prince Kaunitz, to make further changes. After the Seven Years War, he became involved in domestic policy, eventually becoming Chancellor in 1761. It was Kaunitz who partly undid Haugwitz's work in 1760 when he again separated Finance and Commerce from the *Direktorium*, which was now solely responsible for managing the Austrian and Bohemian provinces. Despite the superficial similarities, the *Direktorium* never enjoyed the same centralising role as the Prussian General Directory. Although an improvement on the old system, Austria had not achieved the centralised efficiency Haugwitz had aimed for.

Dissatisfied with the *Direktorium*, Kaunitz instead revived the Council of State to oversee the system of government. This comprised the Chancellor or Chief Minister – Kaunitz himself – and six other senior nobles and bureaucrats. The Council advised the empress on legislation and administration. Whilst not fulfilling any administrative functions itself, it proved to be a useful organ for both advising Maria Theresa and supervising and co-ordinating the work of the various chancelleries (see the chart on page 92). It has been described as 'a kind of parliament of top bureaucrats, with the result that Austria was a bureaucratic absolutism rather than a personal one'.

b) Local Government

Haugwitz's creation of the *Direktorium* led to an extension of bureaucracy into local government. In Charles VI's reign recruitment for the army and tax collection had been managed by the local Diets, and it was this which had formed the basis of their power. Maria Theresa and Haugwitz aimed both to end this power and to increase the income of the state. They were careful to minimise opposition from the Estates by introducing changes gradually.

In each of the ten provinces which made up the Austrian and Bohemian lands, committees of civil servants known as *Repräsanta-tionen* (Representations) were established. These committees, which worked under the *Direktorium*, were at first responsible solely for recruitment into the army and the collection of taxes. Gradually their responsibilities were extended to include road-building, customs duties, and the peasants. Finally, a network of officials, the *Kreishauptman*, was created at local level. Their responsibilities included police, roads, schools, hospitals and providing for the poor. Although they were nominally answerable to the Diets, in practice they took their orders from Vienna. Unlike the practice in Prussia, these officials were usually bureaucrats rather than local nobles. For this reason, and also because they were allowed a greater measure of independence and initiative than their Prussian counterparts, the Austrian system of government at local level was probably more efficient and certainly more sympathetic to the needs of the local peasants than was its Prussian counterpart.

These reforms were resisted, often bitterly, by the local Diets, which saw their functions being steadily undermined. Maria Theresa ignored the protests. When necessary she was prepared to use the army to impose the reforms by force. Both the nature of the reforms and the way in which they were introduced served three useful purposes. The system of administration was made more efficient, the peasants were offered some protection from the nobles, and the power of the nobles was eroded. The nobles recognised this themselves, and by the end of the reign, many were no longer bothering to attend meetings of the Diets, so irrelevant and powerless had these assemblies become.

Outside Austria and Bohemia, Maria Theresa proved to be far more cautious and made few attempts to introduce the reforms she pursued in Austria itself. In the case of the Netherlands, this policy was understandable. They were geographically separated from the rest of the empire. The province was one of her most prosperous possessions after the loss of Silesia, and it contributed a large proportion of her taxes. Maria Theresa saw no reason, therefore, to change the system of government, which was dominated by the local nobles in their Diets.

Hungary exemplified the problems that could occur when the nobility was allowed to control government. All power was concentrated in the hands of a small number of nobles in their Diets. They showed no inclination to contribute more than a token amount to either Maria Theresa's exchequer or her army. Faced with this major problem, Maria Theresa left the Hungarians alone. This was partly because she had been obliged in 1741 to confirm the privileges of the Hungarian nobility, in return for their support against Frederick of Prussia. As a result, none of her reforms were extended to Hungary, whose nobility remained well satisfied with the state of affairs. If there were no revolts during Maria Theresa's reign, that was only because she never gave them any cause to rebel. Maria Theresa's policy towards Hungary was so cautious as to be virtually non-existent.

3 Tax Reform

Closely linked to the reform of government and the need to strengthen the state was a change to the tax system. Haugwitz gave this high priority in his reforms. He estimated that in order to create an army of 100,000 strong – the minimum needed to defend a state the size of Austria – expenditure on the army would have to increase from 9 to 14 million florins a year. Reform of the tax system could also be used to end the government's dependence on the Estates which before 1740 controlled both the level and the collection of taxation. Taking the collection of taxes away from the Diets would both increase government revenues and allow reform of local government.

In 1748 a package of reforms was offered to the Estates. Each estate in Austria and Bohemia would still vote its own taxes, but only once every ten years instead of annually. Collection of taxes and provisions for the army would be organised by civil servants rather than the Estates. New tax registers would be drawn up and the nobles and clergy would pay taxes for the first time, although at only half the rate paid by

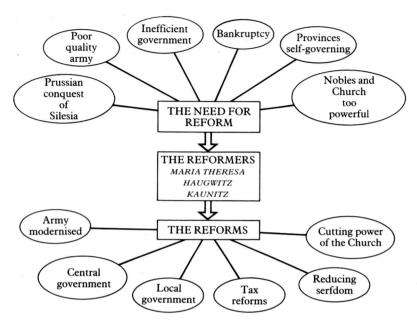

Summary – Maria Theresa: Reforming the Austrian Empire

the peasants. This reform aroused predictable opposition from the Estates. It was opposed both on principle, since the nobility and clergy had never previously been required to pay any taxes, and on the practical grounds that it would deprive the Diets of their power to levy and collect taxes. However, Maria Theresa was able to overcome all the protests. Prussia's conquest of Silesia made it difficult to resist the logic of Haugwitz's proposal. The Estates could not deny that the state needed more taxes in order to protect its territory from further Prussian aggression. It is therefore arguable that Frederick's invasion of Silesia was a blessing in disguise for Maria Theresa, since without it it is doubtful whether she could have persuaded the Estates to accept this crucial reduction in their power. Nevertheless, it was three years before all but one of the Estates accepted the proposals. Carinthia, the remaining defiant Estate, had the new system imposed by decree and enforced by the army.

It cannot be claimed that the new system was successful in solving the empire's financial problems. It is true that there was a substantial increase in government revenue from taxation, which doubled from 20 to 40 million thalers a year between 1745 and 1754. Whilst this was sufficient to meet Haugwitz's wish for a peacetime expenditure on the army of 14 million thalers a year, it was still woefully insufficient for the demands of war. By 1762 the government was again bankrupt, and Maria Theresa was forced to sue for peace just when Frederick's own bankruptcy made him vulnerable. Her financial situation was not helped either by her lavish expenditure on court – some 650 million thalers during her reign. In 1780 her son inherited a debt of 376 million thalers.

Whilst it is true that Austria was one of the few states where the nobles and clergy were taxed, Maria Theresa's financial reforms were piecemeal and, in total, unsuccessful. There were a number of reasons for this. The most important was that the reforms were once again restricted to Austria and Bohemia. In Hungary, taxes were levied at less than half the rate of Austria. The Hungarian Diet retained complete control of its own tax collection and army recruitment and refused all Maria Theresa's requests for increased contributions. The empress felt that she lacked both the power and the moral right to impose tax reform on the Hungarians. This was because at the start of her reign she had been obliged solemnly to swear to uphold all the existing rights and privileges of the Hungarian Diet. She would not consider breaking this oath, however much hardship this imposed on her Treasury, for she felt strongly that it was her honour which distinguished her from rulers like Frederick who did not hesitate to break solemn treaties. Such adherence to principle caused her son to despair, and helps explain both her continuing financial problems and the reason why Maria Theresa was never able to enjoy Frederick's political power.

4 Reform of the Army

The weakness of the Austrian army had already been advertised by its dismal performance in the war against Turkey in the 1730s. The War of Austrian Succession gave further evidence of the need for a radical reform of the army if the Habsburg Empire was to survive as a Great Power. Haugwitz did his best to provide the necessary finances for an expanded army, but what was also needed was an overhaul of its training, equipment and recruitment. As a female ruler, Maria Theresa could not personally undertake this task, although she was keenly interested in army reform and was willing to give it high priority.

Unfortunately, the obvious person to reform the army proved unfit for the task. Maria Theresa's husband, Francis of Lorraine, was amiable but incompetent. Despite his obvious limitations, Maria Theresa was devoted to him, writing him passionate love letters, and tolerating his numerous affairs. The marriage, which resulted in the birth of 16 children in 19 years, proved to be remarkably successful, and Maria Theresa was devastated by his early death in 1765. Perhaps the secret of its success was that, unlike most royal marriages, this was not an arranged marriage between strangers. Francis had known Maria

Theresa since childhood, and it was she who persuaded her father to let her marry the man she loved rather than the son of the Queen of Spain who she had never met.

Unfortunately Francis, though good-humoured, artistic, and a competent administrator and businessman, was no general. Nevertheless, he was given command of the army, and was allowed to retain this position long after it became clear that he was not up to the job. However, when Kaunitz established his new Council of State in 1760, Marshal Daun was made one of the members and was charged with improving the quality of the army.

A number of useful reforms which had been recommended by a Royal Commission in 1748 were at last put into effect. Recruitment was taken out of the hands of the Estates and placed under local officials. Systematic recruitment, based on the Prussian canton system, was introduced, and this made possible a steady expansion in the number of soldiers. New manuals on drill and tactics were introduced and new artillery was developed along with the necessary training for the gunners. The introduction of uniforms gave the army far greater cohesion and *ésprit de corps* and made it easier for commanders to direct their men in battle. Two military academies, one for cadets and one for engineers, were established to improve the skills of the officers.

The result was some improvement, but it was not as great as Maria Theresa would have wished. The army fought much better against Frederick II in the Seven Years War than it had in the War of Austrian Succession, even managing to defeat the formidable Prussian king once or twice. However, the fact remained that the Prussian army continued to demonstrate its superiority in most of the battles, and even when the Austrians did win as at Kunersdorf (see pages 74–5), the commanders proved to be too cautious in following up their victories. Neither the army, nor its commanders matched the quality of their Prussian counterparts. Not until the era of Napoleon was the Austrian army worthy of a great power.

A number of reasons may be offered for the relative lack of success in reforming the army. Maria Theresa showed misplaced loyalty towards commanders she trusted, notably her husband Francis and Marshall Daun. The former was incompetent, while the latter was a fine organiser but was over-cautious in battle. Yet Daun remained responsible for the army, even when there was a younger and more capable commander at hand in Marshal Loudon, who showed his abilities as early as 1758 when he, rather than Daun, forced Frederick II to abandon the siege of Olmutz by ravaging the Prussian supply lines. In addition, the army could never develop as effectively as Prussia's as long as some provinces, notably Hungary, insisted on keeping all recruitment and organisation in their own hands. To make matters worse, army commanders – even Daun himself – had to seek the permission of the *Hofskriegrat* in Vienna before making any offensive moves, and this stifled initiative. Perhaps of greatest signifance was that Daun was trying to reform an antiquated army whilst having to fight off Frederick II, the most formidable general of the eighteenth century. Daun's reforms had gone some way to modernising the Austrian army, but faced with the genius of Frederick II, it remained incapable of recovering Silesia.

5 The Problem of Serfdom

The condition of peasants varied widely within the empire. In a few provinces, such as the Netherlands, serfdom no longer existed. In other provinces it varied in severity. Worst treated were the serfs of Bohemia and Hungary, who were amongst the most depressed serfs in Europe. Here the peasants were obliged to undertake unpaid work for as much as six days a week. This work, usually called the *robot* (from which we get our modern word meaning a machine which works tirelessly for no pay) was supplemented by feudal dues and other obligations to the lord. The nobles dealt with all legal matters to do with the serfs and could impose any punishment short of the death penalty on them. In some provinces the nobles still arranged the marriages of their serfs and could break up families if they wished. It was not unknown for serfs in Bohemia to sell their children in order to pay their taxes. The condition of such serfs was desperate. There were frequent serf revolts, and the inevitability of their defeat and the harsh repression which invariably followed such an episode only underlines how desperate the serfs must have been to undertake revolts in the first place.

Maria Theresa's motives for reform were mixed. Humanitarian feelings were a factor and took her role as 'mother of her people' seriously. This alone would not have induced the empress to challenge the rights of the nobles. More important was her awareness that serfdom was restricting the economic development and hence the strength of her state. As the writer Quesnay summed it up in 1763, 'Poor peasant, poor kingdom; poor kingdom, poor king'. Cautious reform would protect her weakest subjects and allow some improvement of the economy and with it income from taxes. Maria Theresa hoped to achieve this without making any significant change to the existing social system.

She started in 1753 by abolishing the lord's control over peasant marriage. More importantly, a decree of 1769 transferred the responsibility for punishing peasant crimes from the noble to the *Kreishauptman*, and allowed a peasant (in theory at least) to take his noble to court for abusing his power. At the same time the government was negotiating with the various estates to have the *robot* reduced within each province, arguing that the peasant would actually produce more food with more time on his own land. The Austrian estates reluctantly reduced the *robot* to two or three days a week. Meanwhile, Maria

Theresa had abolished serfdom entirely on her own lands as an example to the nobles which, unsurprisingly, they were in no hurry to copy.

If the condition of the Austrian serf was improving, the same could not be said of those in Bohemia and Hungary. Conditions were acute in Bohemia where the combination of war, famine, disease and a nobility whose selfishness exceeded even that of their counterparts in Hungary, combined to produce a crisis in the 1770s. Characteristically, Maria Theresa appointed a Royal Commission to investigate the problem. The Commission raised expectations amongst the peasants that serfdom was about to be abolished entirely, but in fact its recommendation in 1775 was to reduce the *robot* to the Austrian level of three days a week. The refusal of the nobles to accept even this limited reform led to the most savage peasant revolt of Maria Theresa's reign. The revolt was crushed by the Austrian army. It demonstrated to Maria Theresa the need for great caution when introducing reforms, and no further attempts were made to help the peasants for fear of again encouraging their 'unrealistic' expectations.

Maria Theresa had certainly made some moves to protect the serfs, but the experience of Bohemia showed that it was difficult to enforce this in the teeth of noble opposition. The limited reforms she did introduce were largely confined to one small part of her empire and did not apply to the largest single group of serfs, those in Hungary. Although she meant well, there is no real evidence that the serfs of the Austrian Empire were significantly better off in 1780 than they had been in 1740. The condition of the peasants was another weakness that had not been removed, and another problem she left for her son when she died.

6 Religion

Maria Theresa's attitude towards religion was markedly different to the pragmatic and modestly reforming policies she adopted in other areas. This was a subject on which she held inflexible beliefs about her role as a monarch. She still clung to the idea that one of her responsibilities was to protect the Church in her realm. In Maria Theresa's case, her church was the Roman Catholic faith, and she was determined both to protect her Church and to attack rival religions.

Her attitude, which some have suggested was the result of her education at the hands of Jesuit teachers, was likely to cause problems in her multi-national empire. Many of her subjects were Protestants or Jews. Both these minority groups had been persecuted under Charles VI. Indeed, it was the discrimination against them which had led the Silesian Protestants to welcome Frederick II as their liberator in 1740 and to make his conquest so easy and permanent. The eighteenth century had generally seen a reduction in persecution of minority religions. Even 'His Most Catholic Majesty' Louis XV of France could see no purpose in persecuting his Protestant minority. A small but increasing number of states were now practising religious toleration and allowing different faiths to worship without persecution. The fact that they included such successful and prosperous states as Britain, Holland and Prussia offered evidence of the political advantages of toleration.

Maria Theresa's policy of continued persecution is in some ways surprising since it encouraged rather than reduced divisions within her empire and therefore worked against her attempts to strengthen the state. The fact that she persisted in her policies despite the opposition of many of her closest advisers, notably Kaunitz and her eldest son, Joseph, is an indication of how strongly she felt about them. This policy also represents one of the few times where she adopted a similar line to that of her father. One of her strongest statements on religion was made in response to a request from Joseph to be more lenient in her attitude towards the Protestant minority. He wrote,

1 Either freedom of religion, or you drive out of your lands everyone who does not believe as you do. But you cannot do this if you wish to retain excellent workers and good subjects. Have you the right to abuse your power like this? To save souls in spite
5 of them, to coerce their conscience? So long as men obey the state, obey the laws and do not defame Your Majesty – what right do you have to interefere in other things? This is my conviction, and I hope that I will never change my mind.

Maria Theresa was unimpressed by this passionate appeal, and was appalled at what would happen if Joseph came to the throne still holding these views. She replied just as forcefully,

1 There can be nothing more ruinous than your persistence in religious toleration. I still hope, and will not cease to pray, that God will preserve you from such a misfortune, the greatest disaster that could ever afflict this monarchy. In your striving to
5 save useful workers, you will destroy the state and cause the damnation of innumerable souls. What good will it do you to have the true religion when you respect it so little?
   What happens with no dominant religion? Toleration will undermine everything. What other restraint exists? None. I speak
10 politically now, not as a Christian. Nothing is so necessary and beneficial as religion. Would you allow everyone to act as they please? If there was no fixed cult, no subjugation to the church, where would we be? The law of might would take command. Ideas such as yours could cause the greatest misfortune. Think
15 what I suffer when I see your erroneous ways. It is not so much the state that I worry about, but your salvation. I only wish that when I die, I will have the consolation that my son will be as

religious as his forefathers and that he will give up his false
arguments and evil books, and contact with those who have
20 seduced his spirit. Your imaginary freedom could never exist and
would only lead to universal destruction.

With such strongly held views, it is hardly surprising that active
persecution of Protestants continued. Protestants in the Austrian
provinces were either exiled or forced to emigrate – many of them
fleeing to Prussia where Frederick II was only too pleased to have his
state's population increased. A large Protestant community in Moravia
was particularly harshly treated, with the men threatened with conscription and the women and children with prison. Only Joseph's
intervention saved them from this fate.

Maria Theresa would allow no such intercession in the case of the
Jews. She was the last ruler of eighteenth century Europe actively to
persecute the Jews. All the Jews of Bohemia were expelled in 1745, and
in 1777 she revealed how out of touch she was with the increasingly
humanitarian and tolerant attitudes of her time when she refused to
allow Jews to live in Vienna on the grounds that they were an evil race
who were plotting to reduce the people of Austria to beggary.

If Maria Theresa's attitude towards her religious minorities were
hardly designed to help unify her state, the Roman Catholic Church
also found itself under attack. The empress herself sought to protect
her beloved Church – she frequently asserted that her survival in the
War of Austrian Succession was a miracle granted by God because of
her fidelity to the Church. However, Joseph and Kaunitz argued
strongly that the Church was a major constraint on royal power. In 1740
the Church was immensely wealthy and owned sizeable lands. It
organised all the hospitals, poor relief and schools. It enjoyed exemp-
tion from taxation and had its own legal system.

As part of Haugwitz's tax reforms, the clergy were required for the
first time to pay taxes. The rate of tax charged, 1 per cent of income,
was low, but it established the important principle that even a priest
had to contribute a share of his income to the state. The right of
sanctuary and other legal privileges were abolished. Some limits were
placed on monasteries – men could not join them before the age of 24 –
and a few were closed down entirely. The Church lost its control over
hospitals, education and welfare services which were now provided by
the state. The quality of these services noticeably improved. It was no
longer illegal for a Protestant to attend university, although the number
who were able to take advantage of this relaxation were few. The
number of Holy Days was reduced by 24. Censorship of the press and
books was removed from the Church's control. Finally in 1773 the
powerful Jesuit organisation was expelled from the empire. The Jesuits
were one group whom Maria Theresa had particularly tried to protect,
and her failure to prevent their expulsion is evidence that her power was

slipping into the hands of her more aggressive and ambitious son at this time. The fact that the Jesuits had already been expelled from a number of other Catholic states in the years before 1773 made it difficult for Maria Theresa to prevent the same thing happening in Austria.

Reform of the Church had been limited and reluctant. Even after these changes, the Church remained the wealthiest, most privileged and powerful in any European state outside Italy. T.C. Blanning has argued that the fact that reform took place at all is in indication that Maria Theresa was not as prejudiced in the Catholic Church's favour as most historians assert. However, most of the reforms were not introduced until the 1770s. In this, the last period of her reign, her grip on government weakened in both foreign and domestic policies as Joseph's influence was increasing. It is reasonable, therefore, to describe her as a most reluctant reformer when it came to the Roman Catholic Church, and one who sought to protect the one institution which, she believed, held her multi-national state together.

7 Maria Theresa and her Family

In one respect at least, Maria Theresa fulfilled her obligations to her state in a way not achieved by Charles VI, Joseph II or Frederick II, and that was in providing an adult male to succeed her. Maria Theresa had 16 children in all, and took great care both with their education and training, and with finding them suitable husbands and wives. It is one of Maria Theresa's more remarkable achievements that she combined her onerous duties as empress with bringing up her large family. She would not have her children brought up by governesses as was normal in royal families at this time, but put aside time each day to be with her family. As a result, the members of the family were close and devoted to each other. She took care to ensure that her eldest son, Joseph, received all the training he needed, and of which she had been deprived, before he ascended the throne. From 1765, when his father died, Joseph was given a series of important posts, including being appointed co-ruler and Holy Roman Emperor. Whilst these positions did not, in fact, carry as much responsibility as they appeared to (or as Joseph had expected them to), they did mean that Joseph was both experienced in government and confident of exercising his power effectively long before Maria Theresa died in 1780. The long years of apprenticeship were frustrating to Joseph, and help explain the frequent arguments between mother and son in this period, but they were also invaluable experience for the heir-apparent to the Austrian crown.

However, her devotion to her family did not prevent Maria Theresa using her children as pawns in the dynastic marriage game. She played the game with considerable enthusiasm, not appreciating that the days when such alliances could make or break states had passed. The fact that she had been allowed to marry for love did not prevent her

Empress Maria Theresa with her husband and eleven of their sixteen children

returning to the more traditional practice of arranged marriages. Most useful, it seemed, was the marriage of her daughter, Marie-Antoinette, to Louis XVI of France, an act designed to cement the Diplomatic Revolution of 1756 (see pages 64–70). Joseph for his part was obliged to marry a Bavarian princess he detested in the hope that this would prevent future Bavarian claims to the Austrian throne. Several other of Maria Theresa's children were condemned to unhappy marriages as their mother sought to use them to further the ends of her foreign policy.

Maria Theresa worried constantly about her children, and her letters to them are full of good advice and gentle criticisms. She was particularly anxious – with good reason – about two of her children. Marie-Antoinette's frivolity meant that she was becoming unpopular amongst the French people, and Maria Theresa urged her to be more discreet and to show more loyalty to her husband. In the case of Joseph, she feared that his driving ambition would destroy her work and cause unrest among both peasants and nobles. She constantly urged him to follow her cautious pragmatic approach and not to insist on sweeping reforms. Her fears for both proved to be fully justified, but perhaps fortunately she did not live to see their lives end in ruin.

8 Assessment

Maria Theresa's reign had been dominated by the figure of Frederick II. It was he who threatened her state with extinction within weeks of her accession, deprived her of Austria's most valuable province, and who obliged her to institute reforms in order to preserve her state. Both in foreign and domestic policy he dominated her reign, and in many ways Prussia was responsible both for the extent of Maria Theresa's reforms, and her ability to persuade her subjects to accept them.

Faced with the threat from Prussia, Maria Theresa had aimed to strengthen the power and authority of the Austrian state and to extend both the responsibilities of the state to local affairs, and to increase its prosperity. She had no blueprint for a state based on the principles of the Enlightenment, as was fashionable amongst some of her contemporaries as well as her own son. Instead she had instituted reforms only where they were clearly necessary and sought to preserve as much of the old Austrian way of life as was feasible.

Maria Theresa was only too well aware that politics is the art of the possible, and she never tried to do more than was attainable. Bismarck once defined genius as knowing when to stop, and this was one quality Maria Theresa certainly had. Her pragmatism and sense of realism were perhaps her greatest strengths. With only one major exception, she proved to be flexible in her approach to the problems she faced. She was even willing to make modest reforms to her beloved Catholic Church in the interests of the state. Her cautious approach to the nobles and Estates allowed her gradually to increase the power of her state without provoking noble opposition. The one exception was her attitude towards religious toleration, and this is the only area where she showed prejudice. It was the one blind spot in an otherwise realistic and open-minded ruler.

Maria Theresa's personality certainly helped, and she did not hesitate to use it to advantage. Warm-hearted and friendly, she was capable of both charming her ministers who worked for her, and of appealing to ordinary people and nobles, as she demonstrated in Hungary in 1741. In marked contrast with her father, her son or the rulers of Prussia, she was able to gain the trust and affection of her ministers and to work in co-operation with them. With the appointments of Kaunitz and Haugwitz she showed that she could recognise talented individuals and offer them positions of responsibility. On the other hand she showed considerable, not to say excessive, loyalty to other men who did not deserve the positions they held, most notably her husband and Daun. Overall, her style of leadership ensured that the inherently clumsy system of personal monarchy worked reasonably efficiently, and certainly more effectively than it had in her father's reign.

Her success in overcoming the weaknesses of Austria should not be overrated. Her actions were characterised by a caution bordering on ultra-conservatism. Some of her reforms, such as those of central and local government, represented a considerable advance on the previous state of affairs, but were limited to Austria and Bohemia. Others, such as the reform of taxation, religion and the army, were arguably the barest minimum that the Austrian Empire was obliged to undertake faced with Prussian aggression. In some areas, notably the integration of the provinces into a single unified state, she did nothing at all. Such caution did have the merit of preventing any danger of rebellion in Hungary, Netherlands or Milan; on the other hand it also ensured that she would never achieve her stated aim of creating 'systematic order' in her state. Her son Joseph felt frustrated at such slow and modest reforms and by 1780 felt that only the most radical and drastic reforms could make up for the time lost by his mother if Austria was to survive at all.

With the benefit of hindsight, it is easy to point to Maria Theresa's weaknesses and failures. It is by no means as easy to suggest alternative policies which would have been more successful. One person who thought he knew better than Maria Theresa how to run Austria was Joseph. His opportunity to organise Austria more systematically came in 1780. By attempting to impose centralisation, religious toleration and the abolition of serfdom by royal decree, he antagonised many of his subjects. The result was a series of revolts which came close to destroying the Austrian Empire.

Joseph's spectacular failure, which is analysed in the companion Access to History volume *Europe and the Enlightened Despots*, lends credence to the argument that Maria Theresa's cautious approach was the only realistic policy for Austria. However, the argument is not totally convincing, since Joseph's failure can be attributed as much to his methods as to his policies. The question of whether Maria Theresa could and should have achieved more in the way of reform remains open. Historians' views of Maria Theresa are inevitably influenced by their attitude towards Joseph. Biographers of Joseph have tended to point out the limitations to her reforms, and have drawn attention to just how much Joseph still had to do. On the other hand, Maria Theresa's biographers have generally stressed her appalling inheritance and her remarkable achievement in rallying her people when all seemed lost in 1741.

Despite some undoubted achievements, Maria Theresa never reached her goal of a state based on 'Systematic Order'. In 1780 Austria remained less efficient, less unified and less well governed than Prussia. Reform had been limited and often reluctant, but the fact that it happened at all owed much to the realism of Maria Theresa.

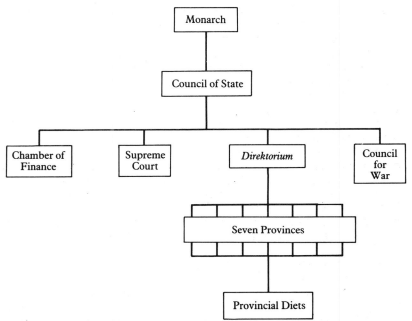

The System of Government in Austria and Bohemia after 1760

Making notes on 'Maria Theresa'

When making notes on this chapter, you will want to keep in mind the main issues involved in Maria Theresa's reign as well as ensuring you have mastered the main events. These issues are: i) What were Maria Theresa's aims? ii) What methods did she use to achieve these aims? iii) How successful was she in achieving her aims? You might feel confident enough in your note-taking to address these issues under each section.

Answering essay questions on 'Maria Theresa'

Essays on Maria Theresa will usually relate only to the material from this chapter. Essays which require a knowledge of her foreign policy are covered in chapter 4. However, it is quite possible that examiners will ask you a question which links Maria Theresa's domestic policy with that of Charles VI. It is also possible that the title may link Maria

Theresa with the work of her son, Joseph II. Comparisons with Joseph II should only be attempted by students who have also studied *Europe and the Enlightened Despots* in this series.

Study the following questions.

1 How successful a leader was Maria Theresa?
2 To what extent did Maria Theresa's problems stem from her father's shortcomings?
3 Were the reforms of Maria Theresa too cautious to be effective?
4 What motives prompted the domestic reforms of Maria Theresa?
5 How far were the domestic policies of Maria Theresa influenced by the loss of Silesia?
6 What was the significance for the Habsburg Empire of Maria Theresa's reforms?

You should be able to identify the main themes that are being asked about in these essays. Which essays are asking you to discuss the *reasons* why Maria Theresa introduced reform? Which essays are asking you to discuss how *successful* her reforms were?

You should note the difference in emphasis between questions 1 and 3. Question 1 is completely neutral; you are asked to make your own judgment on Maria Theresa's success. You should find this fairly straightforward. You will need to examine five or six major aspects of her reign and use the evidence to discuss to what extent her policies achieved her aims or strengthened the state. Your conclusion will summarise both what she achieved, and the limits to her success.

Question 3 is different because the examiner at once announces his/her own judgment: the Empress was not successful because she was too cautious. You will use broadly the same material and topics as you needed for question 1, but must now tailor your material to look specifically at the question of her being over-cautious. Do not assume that you are expected to agree with the examiner's judgment! On the contrary, the examiner is more likely to be impressed with a criticism of the assumptions implied in the title which are well backed up with supporting evidence. Even if you do agree with the essay title – and it would be quite reasonable if you did – you will still have to offer supporting evidence to back up your claim that she was too cautious. What examples do you have where her reforms were made less effective thanks to her caution?

You will find a similar difference in emphasis between question 4 (open-ended and neutral in judgment) and question 5, which asks you to concentrate on one particular reason for reform. You may feel that straightforward questions like 1 and 4 are easier than questions 3 and 5. The latter do have the advantage of both giving you more to discuss, and offering you a focus for your discussion, so that your essay does not become too rambling and wide-ranging.

Finally, question 2 obviously requires some detail on Charles VI's 'shortcomings'. You will need to judge how much of your 45 minutes will be spent on Charles VI's weaknesses, and how much on the problems Maria Theresa had to deal with as a result. The exact proportions probably do not matter too much, provided that there is a balance between the two.

Source based questions on 'Maria Theresa'

1 Maria Theresa's reasons for reform

Carefully study the extracts from Maria Theresa's *Political Testament* on page 88, and then answer the following questions
a) Explain the reference to i) the 'Peace of Dresden' (line 1) and ii) 'holding the balance against France' (line 8). *(4 marks)*
b) Who and what does Maria Theresa blame for the weak state of Austria at this time? *(3 marks)*
c) Comment on Maria Theresa's claims that i) her reforms were based on the 'principle of systematic order' and ii) without her reforms, Austria 'could not survive for long'. *(8 marks)*
d) Does this document satisfactorily explain the reasons for Maria Theresa's reforms of the Habsburg Empire? *(5 marks)*

2 Attitudes towards religious toleration

Carefully study the correspondence between Joseph and Maria Theresa on pages 97 and 98 and then answer the following questions.
a) Comment on the tone of the two sources. Illustrate your answer with examples. *(4 marks)*
b) Why did Maria Theresa think it would be 'the greatest disaster' if Joseph did not change his views on toleration? *(2 marks)*
c) Explain what Maria Theresa meant by 'I speak politically . . . not as a Christian' (lines 9–10)? In what ways does she support her claim that religious toleration was a political question? *(6 marks)*
d) In what ways do these letters help to explain the religious policies that were enacted during Maria Theresa's reign? *(8 marks)*

CHAPTER 6

Frederick II and Prussia

1 Prussia as a Great Power

After 1763 there was no disputing Frederick II's success in defending his people and expanding his territories. Prussia was now firmly established as one of the Great Powers of Europe. Having already impressed the contemporary world by his survival during the Seven Years War, Frederick used the following years to increase his power and prestige further. In 1772 he acquired the valuable province of West Prussia from Poland without a war. Six years later he again went to war with Austria and once again was successful in frustrating Austrian ambitions (see page 134). These events confirmed Prussia as the dominant power in central Europe.

The series of successful wars, combined with a shrewd use of diplomacy (particularly during the 1770s), resulted in an unprecedented growth in the Prussian state. During Frederick II's reign (1740–86), Prussia grew in size from 119,000 to 185,000 square miles. The growth in population was even more impressive. Despite all the ravages of the wars, Prussia's population grew from 2,500,000 to 5,800,000. Of his contemporaries, only Catherine II of Russia could boast comparable achievements – and she never had to face the formidable coalitions with which Frederick had to deal in the Seven Years War.

Frederick had greatly increased the size of his state, turned Prussia into a power respected and feared by the rest of Europe, and established himself as one of the great captains in the history of warfare. His achievements appeared to complement exactly the undramatic but vital groundwork laid down by his father. On closer inspection, however, Frederick's achievements in strengthening his state appear much less clear-cut. How much he really achieved for Prussia, whether he achieved more or less than his father, and his legacy for the future development of Prussia, are all issues which have continued to arouse considerable debate among historians.

2 Law Reform

During the seventeenth century each of Prussia's provinces had its own laws and systems of justice. Since then some steps had been taken to create uniformity. Already during the reign of Frederick William. Samuel von Cocceji had been given responsibility for codifying the laws to give Prussia a single legal system. This work had barely started when Frederick came to the throne, and he encouraged Cocceji to continue with his monumental task. Cocceji was one of the few officials whom

Frederick trusted, and who enjoyed his complete support. Although Cocceji died in 1755, the work continued under other officials. Much of the code was in place by the 1780s, but it was not finally completed until 1794, after Frederick died. The Prussian General Code was published under the name of Frederick William II, but the real authors were Cocceji and Frederick.

Cocceji's reforms gave the provinces of Prussia a common legal system for the first time. In addition, the quality of the judges was improved by paying them salaries. In the past they had received fees from both prosecutor and defendant, and this had inevitably led to the taking of bribes. Judges were to be trained in the law and had to pass examinations before they were eligible to take up a post. All promotion for judges was based on merit and the passing of further examinations. The legal system was made much less complex and the procedure for dealing with appeals was made much quicker, simpler and cheaper. For the first time it was possible for a peasant to take a noble to court and hope to see a fair trial. Cocceji wanted to see the complete separation of the executive from the judiciary. Frederick agreed that he should not interfere in legal matters, and from time to time there were spectacular examples of him accepting legal judgments against himself, particularly in the trivial but famous case where he failed to have a noisy windmill near his palace closed down. But Frederick did not always resist the temptation to intervene. He could, and did, dismiss judges who gave verdicts and sentences he did not like, he imprisoned his own officials without trial, and in the famous case of the miller, Arnold, he insisted on supporting the poor but somewhat unworthy miller against the noble who owned his land, despite repeated rulings by the judges that the miller was in the wrong in his dispute with his lord. This case was an encouragement to all those who saw the king as someone who would protect the humblest citizen against the most powerful of nobles, but it was unfortunate that Frederick chose to ignore the rules of his own legal system, as well as the facts of the case.

Cocceji's legal code opens with a clear statement of intent: 'The welfare of the state and its inhabitants is the object of society. Laws must limit the liberty and rights of the citizen only in the interests of the general good.' However, the reforms were never intended to create equality under the law. Nobles still had their own laws, and they continued to exercise some powers over their serfs. If anything the law reforms increased their power, as they gradually acquired a strong position within the legal profession, which had previously been dominated by the middle class. Nevertheless, Cocceji's reforms were an enormous step forward, giving Prussia one of the fairest and most efficient legal systems in Europe. Equally important was the way in which a common code of laws helped unify the Prussian state. Cocceji's legal system survived almost unchanged until 1900. It was, in fact, Frederick's longest lasting achievement.

3 The System of Government

On the surface it appears that Frederick made no significant changes to the system of government established by his father, and that this was because it proved its value during the wars, when normal government continued with remarkably few problems. Prussia was unique in that the head of state was also the commander-in-chief of the army. The practice of the monarch combining both positions, common in the seventeenth century and before, had long since been abandoned by other states, where the monarchs concentrated on running the government and left the fighting of battles to professional soldiers. But Frederick was the last of the soldier-kings, and the fact that the system of government worked so effectively even when Frederick was away from Berlin campaigning seemed proof that it needed no reforms.

The system of government also suited Frederick because it concentrated all effective power in his hands. Both at central government level, with the General Directory, and at local government level, with the Provincial Chambers, officials were allowed no individual initiative, and all decisions had to be ratified by the entire Directory or Chamber before they could be implemented. It certainly appeared that Frederick was well satisfied with a system which was both efficient and centralised and that he saw no reason to change it.

However, the reality was very different. Although it is true that no changes were made during Frederick's reign to the formal structure of government, they were taking place in the way the system worked in practice. The general impression given of these changes is that Frederick was by no means as satisfied as he appeared to be with the way his government operated. The first of these changes involved the General Directory. During Frederick William I's reign this had been the effective centre of the Prussian government and it had met frequently as a team. Under Frederick II its meetings became less frequent, and it only met with the monarch once a year in a purely formal session. Instead, Frederick increasingly corresponded directly with individual members of the group. This refusal to allow the General Directory to work collectively obviously increased Frederick's own decision-making powers. No individual member either was, or could become, aware of those aspects of government for which he was not directly responsible. Frederick alone, acting as his own prime minister, had access to all relevant information, and only he could make a decision. Increasingly Frederick came to bypass the General Directory, which was allowed to continue as an increasingly irrelevant committee. New and important ministries were established which were not represented on the General Directory, being answerable directly to Frederick. These were: commerce (1741), Silesian affairs (1742) the administration of the army (1746), and forestry (1770).

* At a local level, Frederick continued his father's policy of encourag-

ing the development of a loyal and hard-working civil service. Officials continued to be overwhelmingly recruited from the middle class. Some nobles did become bureaucrats but they enjoyed no special advantages. On the contrary, both entry to government service (which was by examination) and promotion thereafter was based strictly on merit. Senior officials were expected to submit regular reports on their subordinates, and officials hoping for promotion might be interviewed by Frederick himself. Most recruits came from universities where a new subject was introduced for potential government officials. The subject – Cameralism – included law, finance, administration and farming. The first posting for the new official was usually to administer one of the king's own farms. Government officials therefore had a wide knowledge of all aspects of government work before they were given any position of responsibility. For the middle class, with relatively few openings to go into the world of finance and industry, government service offered the best opportunity for security and advancement. Many talented men from outside Prussia, impressed by the high standards of honesty and integrity of the Prussian bureaucracy, were pleased to volunteer to work for the King of Prussia. Frederick had continued to develop his father's bureaucracy, and by the end of his reign Prussia had a civil service which was more efficient, honest and cost-effective than any other in Europe.

Part of the explanation for the high quality of the Prussian civil service was the close personal attention which Frederick devoted to it. He greatly extended the use of Fiscals (see page 44) to spy on his civil servants. Like his father before him, he spent several months each year inspecting his provinces. Local officials would be required to submit their papers and be interviewed by their formidable king. These annual inspections were accompanied by promotions for those who had done well. Those who were found wanting could expect at least instant dismissal, and at worse prison without trial. They had none of the rights to a fair trial that the ordinary citizens of Prussia enjoyed. No doubt it was possible from time to time for officials to persuade Frederick that they were working hard when the reverse was true, or for statistics to be provided which gave the success stories Frederick wanted to hear rather than the truth, but overall his tours of inspection helped ensure a level of honesty and efficiency amongst the relatively small civil service which was the envy of Europe.

The combination of a civil service enjoying some prestige and *ésprit de corps*, recruited from the ablest and most ambitious men both inside and outside of Prussia, with a tight personal control, harsh discipline and a refusal to allow any sort of personal initiative, produced what has been described as the first modern civil service in Europe. This civil service – arguably Frederick's most important contribution to the strengthening of his state – also encouraged those less desirable features of government bureaucracies which have continued to this day. The

Prussian civil service was notorious for its reliance on paperwork and its reluctance to take decisions until ordered to by someone in authority. The Prussian people complained of the 'red tape' with which documents were bound, and the phrase has lasted ever since.

Judgements on Frederick's success in creating an efficient system of government varied both during his lifetime and since his death. Heinitz, who looked after the 'Seventh Department' (Mines) for 25 years, admired Frederick because 'he looked upon his position as a profession and tried to accomplish as much as possible – this alone makes him worthy to be honoured throughout the world'. On the other hand Privy Councillor von Schom claimed that Prussian bureaucrats were actually worse than negro slaves in America, because the Prussians *willingly* accepted despotic and cruel orders. A balanced assessment would agree that Frederick did create Europe's first modern civil service and gave the Prussian people a system of administration which was honest and efficient, but that by stifling all initiative and taking even trivial decisions himself, he was making the whole system too dependent on the personality and work of the monarch. Such a system could only be justified if Frederick ensured his successor was as hard-working as he was.

4 Financial Policies

During the Seven Years War much of Prussia had been devastated and overrun by foreign armies. The existing system of collecting state income had all but collapsed, and Frederick found himself dependent on his British subsidies and the ruthless exploitation of his conquered provinces of Silesia and (temporarily) Saxony. It was no wonder that he fell into despair when Britain ended its subsidies. The return to peace meant that high priority needed to be given to restoring both his shattered state and his tax system. The well-known story of how Frederick brushed aside the congratulations of his ministers when the war ended in 1763, instead demanding precise information on how much money was required to restore Prussia, can be taken as proof of his modesty and the high priority he gave to the welfare of his subjects. Equally it can be taken as evidence of the importance he attached to restoring the strength of his state.

Frederick's financial policies ensured a steady increase in his annual income in the years after 1763. The main taxes under Frederick William had been the Excise and the Land Tax. Frederick made no attempt to extend the Land Tax to nobles outside East Prussia. It is an unusual example of Frederick the centralising and unifying monarch failing to establish a common system throughout his state. The Excise was reorganised and, known as the *Régie* was increased and extended to further items, including meat and alcohol. It was a highly unpopular tax, made even more so by the fact that the collectors were a group of

French Tax-farmers. In addition, Frederick introduced a number of monopolies, particularly on coffee and tobacco. The effect was a significant increase in the cost of these goods. All these changes helped ensure increased revenues for the state, if not increased popularity for tax collectors.

Prussia enjoyed a steadily increasing population – a result of a long period of peace after 1763, steady grain prices, considerable immigration and the acquisition of the two provinces of Silesia and West Prussia. Because of this, the increased duties, and a more efficient system of tax collection, income from taxes rose from 7 to 19 million thalers a year. It was an impressive achievement. It enabled Frederick to finance the continued expansion of his army, to provide funds on a level unmatched by any other ruler for the welfare of his people, to enable him to ensure that he had a surplus over expenditure and never got into debt, and to bequeath his successor an enormous treasure of over 50 million thalers. The significance of Frederick not falling into debt after 1763 cannot be overstressed. He was the only monarch in Europe whose expenditure was less than his income, and he was therefore never in the position, experienced by so many other kings, of having to give up elements of his political power in return for grants of additional taxes from his subjects. There is a clear connection between Frederick's autocratic powers and his solvency.

However, even this financial success story – so central to Frederick's achievements as a monarch – was not without its shortcomings. The increase in the government's income during his reign (171 per cent) was not significantly higher than the increase in population during the same period (132 per cent), suggesting that the real basis of Frederick's increased income was his increased population, rather than the changes he made to the tax system. It is arguable that he might have been expected to increase his income even more than he did, given the increased population. He relied on sources of income – the Excise, Land Tax and customs duties – which were traditional and which tended to discourage trade and enterprise. Nevertheless, there can be no doubt that his financial policies, although lacking in any originality, did strengthen his state.

5 Economic Policies

Frederick's economic policies followed a similar pattern to his ideas on finances. His actions were designed to increase the prosperity and therefore the power of his state, but he followed a generally conservative approach. He accepted that mercantalism was the best method of achieving this, although from the 1770s onwards the theory was being called into question by French and British economists. Frederick tried to develop manufacturing industry by encouraging the immigration of skilled workers, and by exempting factory owners and their workers from various taxes and from conscription. In addition, potential capitalists were often provided with an initial free grant of cash, land and buildings. Considerable emphasis was placed on improving the transport system. The river Oder was made navigable throughout its length by an ambitious programme of dredging, whilst a new canal linked the Oder with the river Havel. Frederick found the acquisition of Silesia in 1740 particularly useful. What had previously been Austria's most industrialised province now became his. Frederick was proud of the continued developments he oversaw in textiles, sawmills, brick works and above all, mining. By the end of his reign, Silesia boasted over 200 coal and iron-ore mines, and the first steelworks in Germany was started there in 1785. With some justification Frederick called this province 'my Peru', after the Spanish colony which provided Spain with so much of its silver, and, in theory, its power.

At one point during the 1760s Frederick seems to have played with the idea of establishing a totally centralised economic system under state control. He established a royal bank, a state insurance company, various state-run trading companies and state factories. At the same time new ministries for commerce, mines and forests were established. Such a policy would have carried mercantilism to its ultimate extent. However, the state-run enterprises were not successful and Frederick's experiment with state capitalism quickly faded away.

Frederick was well pleased with his achievements. By 1786 Prussia had emerged as the fourth most industrialised state in Europe (after England, France and Holland). Around 100,000 people worked in manufacturing, mainly in the textile industry. Thanks partly to heavy duties on imports, there was a favourable trade balance of around 3 million thalers a year. A start had also been made on the development of a Prussian merchant marine fleet, although this did not develop significantly until the reign of Frederick's successor.

However, despite the fact that Prussian industry provided his army with equipment and kept his trade balance in the black, some serious weaknesses remained. Frederick constantly complained that the Prussians were uninterested in industry and he remained heavily reliant on foreign investment and capitalists for its development. And, whilst Prussia was developing some industry, it remained overwhelmingly an agricultural state, and was actually falling behind the rapidly developing commercial and industrial economies of England and France. There are a number of explanations for the failure of the Prussian economy to develop more rapidly than it did. The rigid Prussian social system and the continued existence of serfdom conspired to deprive Prussia of potential industrial workers. Ambitious members of the middle class were encouraged to work in government service rather than industry. In his search for immediate financial gain, Frederick retained a number of internal customs barriers and levied heavy duties on goods through the hated *Régie*. This had the effect of increasing prices and discouraging demand. Frederick's economic policies allowed a modest industrial and trading expansion. This was sufficient for his purposes, but as with his attitude to finances and government, he showed a marked reluctance to tamper with systems established by his father.

6 Social Policies

Frederick adopted a paternalistic attitude towards his subjects, and was prepared to spend considerable sums of money on reforms which would ensure a basic standard of living and prevent the danger of revolt or starvation. This was particularly evident in the years following 1763. Faced with the devastation of the recent wars, he gave about 40 million thalers in grants and loans to landowners to enable them to restock their farms. In similar fashion, he introduced state granaries to help stabilise the price of corn. The state bought corn when it was plentiful and sold it cheaply when it was in short supply. This helped keep prices stable and removed the fear of famine from his people. It was a strikingly successful example of state paternalism, and the lack of any serf revolts during his reign is in marked contrast with the frequent revolts in Austria, Poland and Russia. However, Frederick was not interested in helping his people as an end in itself. In fact he despised his own subjects and regretted the fact that fate meant he was destined to rule such an unworthy people as the Prussians, rather than the more civilised French. This makes an interesting contrast with his father, who intensely disliked the French and who, for all his brutality, actually wanted to be liked by his subjects.

In the field of education, a law of 1763 decreed compulsory education for all children of primary school age. However, little was actually achieved. Although a number of schools were built, there was a constant shortage of teachers, probably because they were so badly paid. Frederick even resorted to employing discharged soldiers as schoolmasters. Unfortunately these teachers were frequently no more literate than the children they were supposed to teach. Like his father, Frederick found that passing laws on education meant little without adequate funding.

It is perhaps significant that there was one province in which a real attempt was made to improve the education system. After Prussia acquired West Prussia from Poland in 1772, considerable effort was made to improve the quality of schooling for the largely Polish population. Within three years about 750 schools were built in the province. Teachers were expected to speak both Polish and German. Why then did Frederick, who generally neglected education, pay particular attention to it in this one area? The answer is that, as a newly acquired province with a largely 'foreign' (Polish) population, Frederick considered it essential to integrate it as quickly as possible. The example of West Prussia, sometimes used to demonstrate that

Frederick had a real commitment to improving the standard of education in Prussia, in reality underlines the main principle of his education policies – that they were another means of strengthening and unifying the state.

7 The Nobles and the Peasantry

The Prussian nobility was a small group, numbering around 1 per cent of the total population of the state. Frederick William had not completely trusted them and in general their power had been restricted to control over their peasants and the filling of bureaucratic jobs at a local level. Frederick took a different view. He saw the nobles as essential partners in governing Prussia. This partly reflected his awareness that the nobility had largely lost any wish to limit royal power. He knew that the increasing financial difficulties faced by many nobles meant that they now often looked to the state to provide paid employment for their younger sons. Frederick's favourable attitude towards the nobility also reflected his own conservatism. Only the nobles, he said, had the necessary upbringing and 'honour' to be given positions of real responsibility.

The nobles benefited from Frederick's rule in a number of ways. He openly favoured them as army officers. During the Seven Years War the appalling losses had obliged him to use increasing numbers of middle-class men as officers. But once the war was over, these were gradually dismissed, regardless of their ability, and replaced by nobles, however inexperienced. This was a striking exception to Frederick's usual rule of promotion on merit. By 1786 only 10 per cent of officers were non-nobles, and nearly all of these held junior ranks in the least glamorous regiments. He had effectively closed off one opportunity for the middle class to advance themselves.

Frederick showed his support for the nobles in other ways. He did not extend the Land Tax to all nobles, as many observers expected, and he supported them rather than the peasants when it came to restoring agriculture after the Seven Years War. It was the nobles who received the bulk of the subsidies, and he created a scheme whereby nobles, but not peasants, could borrow money at a low rate of interest to improve their farms. Only nobles could become Presidents of the Provincial Chambers, and Frederick increased their importance by corresponding directly with them rather than through their nominal master, the General Directory. Similarly, only nobles could become *Landrats*, the local officials responsible for rural areas. The law reforms of Cocceji also bolstered their position. Their status was given legal recognition and protection, they retained their legal powers over their serfs and they were still responsible for collecting taxes and conscripting men to the army. They were also given legal protection from abuses of power by the government, and at the same time a new profession was opened up to them – the judiciary – which had previously been monopolised by an oligarchy of middle-class lawyers. In addition, Frederick encouraged the establishment of *Landschaften* (Rural Credit Associations). These local groups of nobles existed nominally to discuss agricultural problems, but Frederick encouraged them to discuss other matters, and to a certain extent they replaced the discredited Diets as the forum in which nobles could air their views. Finally, Frederick made it almost impossible for members of the middle-class to become nobles. The only men he ennobled were the few who distinguished themselves on the battlefield. Nobles were forbidden to engage in commerce or trade, whilst the middle class were prevented from becoming landowners. In these ways he reduced social mobility and helped return the nobility to a self-perpetuating caste.

Frederick summed up his attitude to the nobles in his *Political Testament* of 1752.

1 The policy of the sovereign of this state is to preserve the noble
  class, who form the finest jewel in his crown. To enable them to
  maintain themselves in their possessions, it is necessary to
  prevent others from acquiring noble estates and to compel them
5 to put money into commerce instead. Other social groups may be
  wealthier, but none can surpass the nobles in valour or loyalty
  . . . . It is also necessary to prevent noblemen from taking service
  abroad, to inspire them with an *ésprit de corps* and a national
  spirit.

By 1786 the nobles had regained the dominant position in Prussia they had enjoyed a century before. Openly favoured and flattered by Frederick, unlike the middle-class bureaucrats whom he so obviously distrusted, and in control of many of the top jobs in the General Directory, the Provincial Chambers, the judiciary and army, they continued to exercise wide powers over their peasants. Only in the bureaucracy itself was the middle class strongly represented, where promotion was based strictly on merit, and the noble was in effect disadvantaged. Prussia was becoming a state in which rigid social divisions were enforced. This was all part of Frederick's plan to give the nobles a real stake in Prussia and to wean them effectively from their former loyalties to their own localities. In this he was successful. Nobles came increasingly to identify themselves with Prussia and to dominate the government, a pattern which was to continue until 1945.

* By contrast, Frederick did little to help the peasants. No attempt was made to abolish or reduce the burdens of serfdom, other than on royal lands. Help for the peasants was limited to the introduction of state granaries. Frederick had good reason to be cautious about helping the peasants. If he had done so he would have antagonised the nobles, the one class whose support he felt he really needed. He might also have risked civil unrest, and would certainly have risked the whole system of

army recruitment upon which the continued existence of Prussia depended. Once again his *Political Testament* provides evidence of his attitude towards the peasants – and of the hopes which never materialised.

> 1 I have relaxed on royal lands the services which peasants have to
> perform. Instead of six days a week, they now only work three.
> This has provoked the nobles' peasants. The sovereign should
> hold the balance evenly between the peasant and the gentleman,
> 5 so they do not ruin each other. . . . One will have to free the serfs
> in due course. . . . One should prevent the peasants from buying
> nobles' land and nobles buying peasants' land, because peasants
> cannot serve as officers in the army, and if the nobles [buy up]
> peasant holdings, they diminish the number of inhabitants and
> 10 cultivators.

The continued existence of serfdom was not in Prussia's long-term interests, and Frederick knew it. However, the short-term need for stability and the need not to antagonise the nobility explain his failure to tackle the problem. It would be left to a later generation of Prussian rulers to abolish the institution and finally bring Prussia into the modern world. Like his father, Frederick did not feel strong enough to challenge the power of the nobles. The failure of both monarchs to tackle the major problem meant that Prussian development was held back by an outdated social and economic system. They had maintained social peace, but had failed to strengthen the state in one crucial area.

8 The Army and the State

The army was the most important institution in Prussia. It was the instrument which had enabled successive kings to unite scattered and disunited provinces, to protect the open borders from attack and, under Frederick, to turn his basically poor state into a great power. Already under Frederick William, the army had swollen to an enormous size and had enjoyed exceptional prestige in the state. Under Frederick, this tendency was further increased.

Frederick continued to lavish resources on his army after 1763. It continued to expand in size and to have a high proportion – usually 70 per cent – of tax revenue spent on it. By 1786 it had grown from 87,000 to 200,000 men. In this year Prussia was the thirteenth largest state in Europe in terms of population, the tenth in terms of area, but the third in size of army. Only the Russian and French armies were larger. Apart from the brief War of Bavarian Succession of 1778–9, Frederick never again had to use his army in battle. Instead, its very existence, combined with his enormous prestige as the greatest general of his age, were to act as a deterrent. Its effectiveness is indicated by the fact that neither Austria nor her allies made any further attempt after 1763 to regain Silesia.

The reputation of his army is also indicated by the speed with which other states remodelled their armies on Prussian lines. These states included his defeated enemies, Russia, Austria and France as well as his former ally, Great Britain. Perhaps most remarkably of all, Prussian influence extended to the United States army whose success in the War of American Independence (1776–83) owed much to the training and organisation of a Prussian officer, Steuben.

Frederick emphasised the importance of the army in every way he could. Prussia was unique in that it was the one state in Europe where the only way to achieve noble status was through the army. In 1763 he wrote:

1 Let me make it plain for once and for all, that I will not sell titles or noble land for money and thereby debase my nobility. Noble status may only be gained by the sword and by bravery. I will only choose to raise to the estate of nobility those vassals who are 5 capable of rendering to me useful service in the army.

The well-justified prestige of the army, Frederick's policy of openly favouring army officers over civilians, the lavish expenditure, and the way he restricted real honour to those who fought for him, all helped create a state of mind in Prussia where militarism became a popular and potent force. Prussia was the most militaristic state in Europe. Uncritical admiration for the army and its achievements and values was one of the more unfortunate legacies that Frederick left future generations of Prussians.

* Such a high status for the army would have been justified had the army retained the skill and efficiency it had displayed so often in the first 23 years of Frederick's reign. However, after 1763 the Prussian army went into decline, and the evidence was there for all to see. As early as 1778, in the War of Bavarian Succession (see page 134), the Prussian army had performed feebly, and Frederick had been glad to sign a quick peace treaty, although Prussia made no territorial gains. Frederick was aware that his army was no longer the potent force it had once been, but he never seriously addressed the problem. After he died the army continued to decline in quality, if not in size or in complacency. It again performed badly fighting the French between 1792 and 1795, before it was destroyed with ease by Napoleon in a single day at the battle of Jena in October 1806. Prussia proved to be the easiest of Napoleon's many victims. Napoleon visited Frederick's tomb after the battle of Jena and was kind enough to say 'Hats off gentlemen! If he were still alive, we would not be here now'. This flattery was quite unjustified, because Napoleon had just defeated an army led by Frederick's old officers and fighting with his methods.

Frederick II of Prussia

With the benefit of hindsight, it is not difficult to point to the causes of the decline of the Prussian military. Frederick made no attempt to modernise his army, being content to continue with the tactics and organisation which had served him so well in earlier wars. Frederick and his father together turned the Prussian army into the most formidable military machine Europe had ever seen. And Frederick himself must take the responsibility for failing to prevent its decline after 1763. Even the finest generals, it seems, are not always the best men to manage an army in peacetime.

9 Frederick and his Successors

Mirabeau, who visited Prussia in 1785, predicted that the mighty Prussian state would collapse once Frederick died. Frederick himself shared this view. He had been married in the 1730s, but refused to live with his wife and treated her throughout their long marriage with cold contempt, to the point where he even refused to allow her to say goodbye to him when he lay dying on the grounds that he was too busy! He had no children, and had therefore failed to fulfil one of the duties of the monarch, that of perpetuating his line with a male heir. Fortunately there was no shortage of brothers and nephews, so there was never a danger of the Hohenzollern male line dying out, or of a war of Prussian Succession to match the recent War of Austrian Succession. Unfortunately, the heir was Frederick's nephew, Frederick William, rather than Frederick's talented younger brother, Henry.

Frederick had no illusions about his successor. 'Let me tell you how it will be after my death', he confided to a friend, 'There will be merriment at court, my nephew will squander the treasure and allow the army to degenerate. His women will then govern and the state will go to rack and ruin'. Frederick's gloomy predictions proved to be correct. Frederick William was amiable, not without some ability – like Frederick he was an accomplished musician – but he was also extravagant, sought easy popularity, and lavished enormous sums of money on Wilhelmina Encke, who had been his mistress since she was 14 years old. Frederick William, above all, disliked the work of government, and it was his tragedy that he was born to rule a state where the monarch took all the decisions. As a result of his indolence, the country drifted rudderless and real power fell into the hands of a group of unscrupulous courtiers, including Wilhelmina and her husband. The influence of Wilhelmina was particularly ironic, since Frederick during his lifetime had always denounced with particular anger the influence of the royal 'whores' in other states. Frederick William's reign did see some useful reforms introduced, notably the final implementation of Cocceji's legal reforms in 1794, but it also saw Prussia involved in a disastrous war with France (1792–5) and diverted into two more Partitions of Poland (1793–5). By the end of his reign in 1797 he was 55 million thalers in debt, and the nobles were taking increasing power from the unresisting hands of the king.

Frederick William II was succeeded by his son, Frederick William III. An honourable and honest man who lived much more frugally than his father, and who was faithfully married to his wife, he was nevertheless too much in awe of his famous great-uncle (whom he had known as a child) even to consider changing his system of government. Like Frederick William II, he lacked the capacity for hard work to oversee the administration, and Prussia continued to slide into a genteel decline whilst living on Frederick's reputation. The sorry state of

Prussia only became apparent to all to see when on 14 October 1806 Napoleon smashed the vaunted Prussian army with contemptuous ease at the twin battles of Jena and Auerstadt.

* To what extent should Frederick himself bear the responsibility for the later decline of Prussia? At first sight it may appear unreasonable to attach any blame to him. How far is it valid to criticise any ruler for what happens twenty years after his death? It is certainly true that Frederick can not be held responsible for the actions of Frederick William III, whom he hardly knew. Nor can he be blamed if his successors were so overwhelmed by his reputation that they dared not touch any of his institutions – after all Frederick had spent his lifetime discouraging such hero-worship from his subjects. The real accusation against him involves two charges – that he continued a system which relied totally on the personality and hard work of the king, and that he failed to train his successor, Frederick William II.

All Frederick did for his successor was to write him two *Political Testaments* and leave him a treasure of 50 million thalers. The *Testaments* are very useful for historians. Since they were never intended to be published, they provide what is probably a genuine insight into Frederick's real aims and hopes. But Frederick knew that they were not worth the paper they were written on unless he obliged his nephew to undertake some real training before he succeeded to the throne. This he conspicuously failed to do. Frederick William was given neither military nor government responsibilities. Instead, Frederick merely grumbled to his friends that his nephew would make a poor king. It is also significant that, knowing he had an inadequate successor and (presumably) feeling it was not even worth attempting to teach him his responsibilities, Frederick also failed to change his system to make it flexible enough to cope with a king who did not wish to rule. That, of course, would have involved creating an independent central government and giving some initiative and responsibility to local officials. The intriguing possibility exists that Frederick's failure either to reform the army or the system of government was because he did not care what happened after his death. If this is the case, it inevitably raises the question of whether Frederick's work in strengthening the Prussian state was motivated more by personal ambition than the long-term development of Prussia.

Any discussion on Frederick's success in strengthening his state must take into account the extent to which he was responsible for the disaster of 1806. The ease with which Napoleon destroyed old Prussia suggests that the apparent strength of Frederick's regime was illusory and too dependent on the hard work of the monarch himself. Obviously some of the responsibility for the collapse also belongs to the monarchs who succeeded him, but the fact remains that it was Frederick the Great's Prussia which fell to pieces in a single day in October 1806.

10 Conclusion

Both Frederick William I and Frederick II contributed greatly to the development of Prussia during the eighteenth century. Despite their apparent differences of temperament and attitude, they shared a common approach to their subjects and adopted similar policies in most areas. Frederick William and his son both had clear aims for their state. In the case of Frederick William, his simplistic statements about his powers (see page 34) provided a framework for the power he exercised. He was particularly influenced by his religious faith, and felt that God had chosen him to be ruler of Prussia. He was in fact one of the last believers in the Divine Right of Kings.

Frederick II took a cynical view of religion. So uninterested was he in spiritual matters that he asked to be buried next to his dogs in the garden of his favourite palace, rather than in a church. His wish was not finally achieved until 1991. Nevertheless, his philosophy of government, although shorn of religious principles, was remarkably similar to that of his father. In his *Essai sur les Formes de Gouvernement* (1771), he wrote his famous summary of the role of the monarch.

1 The ruler must remind himself that he is a man like the least of
   his subjects – the first judge, the first general, the first financier,
   the first minister. He is only the first servant of the state, obliged
   to act as if at any moment he had to render an account of his
5 administration to the citizens. He is the head of the family. With
   the best will in the world he can make mistakes. Therefore in
   governing, as with everything else, we must be content with what
   is least defective.

*Frederick William was more innovative than his son in his domestic policy. He clearly identified the areas that were needed for the development of his state – a strong army, sound finances and an efficient centralised system of government – and introduced major reforms to all three. The success of his reforms is indicated by Prussia's survival during the wars of 1740–63. Frederick II was aware of the limits to the quality of both his army and system of government by the end of his reign, but he showed himself reluctant to change a system which had worked so well. Only in a few areas of domestic policy did Frederick introduce more changes than had his father. The introduction of state granaries and Cocceji's reforms of the legal codes were important innovations with significant benefits for Prussia. Apart from these, Frederick II proved to be both less innovative and more complacent in his domestic policy than his father.

Both father and son had a similarly paternalistic attitude towards their subjects, the same preference for the realities of power rather than the superficiality of court life, and the same meanness when it came to spending money on themselves or their courtiers. Both devoted their lives tirelessly to managing the government personally, and both spent several months a year travelling around their provinces inspecting the work of their officials. This personal style of government was unique among the major powers of Europe, and was not adopted by any of the later rulers of Prussia. Whether it was in fact the best use of their time is questionable. But since neither entrusted any real power or responsibility to ministers, it was probably the only way they could ensure that their orders were obeyed. Nor was it just ministers whom they distrusted. Both men shared a cynical view of mankind, and neither expected any thanks or gratitude from their subjects for all the hard work they did. This is a reminder that both men saw their role as strengthening the Prussian *state*, and not the Prussian people. Despite the apparent differences in their attitude towards religion, they both adopted the practice of religious toleration, which certainly helped strengthen the Prussian state by encouraging a steady stream of immigrants into the less populated areas.

Both men share the responsibility for some of the weaknesses which existed in the Prussian state. It was Frederick William who created a system of government that relied totally on the will of the monarch, and who discouraged all initiative and independence by officials and ministers alike. Frederick continued with this inefficient system of government but added to it a reliance on the nobles which further undermined the effectiveness of what was theoretically an absolute monarchy.

There were some differences in their approach. Frederick William was far more conscious of his obligation to provide an heir capable of ruling the state effectively. He ensured that his son was given a thorough training in administration and the army before he became king. Although Frederick, who disliked this training at the time, later acknowledged how important it had been to him, he showed none of the same concern about training his successor in turn, with disastrous long-term consequences. Frederick's lack of interest in what happened after he died is perhaps the most striking departure from his father's approach. They also differed in their attitude towards the nobles, with Frederick William seeing them as just another group to be controlled under state power, whilst Frederick wanted them to be his partners, if subordinate partners, in the running of Prussia.

A comparison restricted to domestic policies would suggest Frederick William did far more to strengthen the state. He turned a scattered group of territories into one of the potentially most formidable powers in Europe. By contrast, Frederick II was content, with few exceptions, to accept uncritically his father's policies, even when they were evidently losing their effectiveness. His task was much easier, since he inherited a state which already enjoyed an efficient system of government, sound finances and unchallenged royal power.

However, limiting the comparison to domestic policies is misleading. In the eighteenth century it was military success which was the main criterion for judging the strength of a state. It was in this field of diplomacy and war that Frederick excelled and it was here that Frederick William proved to be less than competent. It was Frederick's skill as a general and diplomat which gained the valuable provinces of Silesia and West Prussia. By the standards of his age, it was Frederick who was the successful ruler. Today we may feel that Frederick William's unexciting domestic reforms were more important in building up Prussia than Frederick's expensive wars, but the eighteenth century had different values. By the standards of the age, Frederick William had done little for his state. It was Frederick who was the 'great' ruler, and they awarded him the title.

In the final analysis, Prussian power depended on the strength of the army. More than most other states, Prussia's geography meant that it would rise and fall through the capabilities of its armed forces. Frederick William created the formidable military machine but did not know how to use it. His son made brilliant use of the army, adding to its strength his own genius as a general, but he failed to keep it up-to-date during the last years of his reign.

Both men contributed significantly to the strengthening of Prussia during the eighteenth century. Together they turned Prussia into one of the Great Powers of Europe. But both men were also responsible for creating a system of government that was too rigid and too personal. Faced with the challenge of the French Revolution and Napoleon, it was the apparently strong Prussia which collapsed whilst the apparently weaker Austria survived. The events of October 1806 demonstrated both how dependent Prussia remained on the personality of its monarch, and how fragile its apparent strength was.

Making notes on 'Frederick II and Prussia'

Your notes should try to identify those aspects of Frederick's domestic policies which strengthened his state, and those which weakened it. Note that you are not expected to judge Frederick on what he did for his people. No ruler at this time saw his duty in terms solely of benefiting his people, and Frederick was not alone in seeing both his own and his people's work as being for the good of Prussia.

You might find it helpful to divide your page into two columns, summarising in one those actions which strengthened his state, and in the other those that weakened it. Some of his policies will clearly belong in one column or the other, but there are a number, such as the civil service, where comments will go into both columns. This table should

SUCCESSES	FAILURES
Law Reform	Not completed until 1794
Effective personal government	System of government unreformed
Efficient Civil Service	Excessive bureaucracy
Efficient tax system	Tax system unreformed
Economy developed	Mercantalist system retained
State granaries	Serfdom unreformed
Education decree	Decree ineffective
Nobles given status	Nobles given excessive power
Finest army in Europe	Army declined after 1763
Left 8 million Thalers to successor	Failed to train successor
Rossbach and Leuthen, 1757	Jena, 1806

Summary – Frederick II and Prussia

give you a useful summary to help judge his overall contribution to the development of Prussia.

The following gives a possible list of topics for your summary table.

1 Defending the state from foreign invasion
2 Strong army
3 Legal system
4 Preventing starvation
5 Preventing social unrest
6 System of government
7 Tax system
8 Economic development

9 Social Reform
10 Religious policies
11 Nobles and serfs
12 Training an heir

You are now ready to compare the achievements of Frederick and Frederick William. You should avoid falling into the trap of over-simplifying what they did for Prussia by asserting that Frederick William's work was all good and successful, whilst his son threw away his inheritance through his wars and complacency. Using the Conclusion to this chapter and your notes on chapter 3, you can draw up a similar table for Frederick William. This should clearly indicate that both men had successes and failures in their attempts to strengthen the state.

Answering essay questions on 'Frederick II and Prussia'

Essay questions on Frederick II can be divided into four main groups:
i)   Those which deal solely with his foreign policy and wars; these are discussed in chapter 4.
ii) Those which compare his achievements with those of Frederick William I.
iii) Those which discuss his domestic policy alone.
iv) Those which require an overall assessment comparing his foreign policy and domestic achievements.

It is the second, third and fourth groups of questions which are discussed here. Note that you are unlikely to be asked to compare Frederick II with Maria Theresa.

Study these questions
1 Do you agree that Frederick William I contributed more to the development of Prussia than Frederick the Great?
2 To what extent was Frederick II indebted to his father for his success?
3 Compare the strengths and weaknesses of Prussia in 1740 and 1786.
4 Do you agree that Frederick II 'pursued aggrandisement at the cost of improvement'?
5 'A first rate military leader, but a second rate ruler'. How valid is this judgement of Frederick II?
6 In what ways, if any, was Frederick II an innovator in his domestic policy?

These are fairly typical of the type of question you might have to answer. The first three ask for comparisons between Frederick II and his father. Questions 1 and 2 are explicit on this, question 3 rather less so.

Whenever you are faced with comparative questions such as 1 and 2, you have to decide whether it is better to adopt a chronological approach – ie, going through the reign of Frederick William, pointing out all his achievements (and failures), then doing the same for Frederick II and ending with a conclusion tying it all together – or whether to adopt a thematic approach. This means going through each of the main factors which made a state strong and comparing the achievements of each ruler within each paragraph.

The second method is harder but by far the more effective. Armed with your summary tables, you should feel able to tackle the essays this way. However, you will not be able to cover all the 13 headings as separate paragraphs. Which five or six will you concentrate on? (You may be able to combine some into a single paragraph).

Questions 4 and 5 deal with Frederick II only. They offer a direct link between Frederick's successes as a general with his 'failure' in domestic policy. You will need to look at the evidence from chapter 4 in addition to this chapter. You will need to make some sort of judgement about how you are going to balance your essay between domestic policies and wars. You will clearly not have time to cover both in detail, and you will therefore need to be quite ruthless in eliminating irrelevant material, and only discussing aspects of his policies which will help you to answer the question most directly.

You should have spotted that question 6, although not mentioning Frederick William by name, will require some awareness of his contribution. In your plan you should divide Frederick II's domestic policies into two groups – those that were innovative, and those which merely continued what Frederick William started. Whilst you are likely to end up generally agreeing with the examiner, you should put some emphasis on those policies which Frederick did originate himself. Which ones are these?

Source-based questions on 'Frederick II and Prussia'

1 Frederick's Aims
Carefully read Frederick's statement of aims on page 121. Answer the following questions.
a) Explain the phrase 'first servant of the state' (line 3). (2 marks)
b) What impression was Frederick trying to give about, i) his aims for his people, and ii) the limits to his power? (6 marks)
c) In what ways does the fact that this source comes from a book published during Frederick's lifetime affect its reliability as evidence about his aims? Explain your answer. (6 marks)
d) Using this source and your own knowledge, discuss the view that Frederick shared the same aims as his father. (6 marks)

2 Social Class in Prussia

Carefully read Frederick's comments on the nobles (page 115), the peasants (page 116) and the army (page 117). Answer the following questions.

a) Explain the phrases i) 'provoked the nobles' peasants' (page 116 line 3), and ii) 'debase my nobility' (page 115 line 2) *(4 marks)*

b) In what ways did Frederick claim he was protecting the peasants? How accurate were his claims? *(4 marks)*

c) These sources come from private documents, not intended for publication. How does this affect their probable reliability? Explain your answer using examples from the sources. *(6 marks)*

d) To what extent do these sources provide a satisfactory explanation for Frederick's failure to abolish serfdom? *(6 marks)*

CHAPTER 7

Austria and Prussia after 1763

1 Prussian and Austrian Foreign Policy Aims in 1763

In 1763 Frederick II appeared to be at the pinnacle of his success in foreign affairs. Prussia had gained Silesia, successfully challenged Austrian domination of the Holy Roman Empire and had joined the ranks of the Great Powers. Frederick's basic aim was to hold on to these gains, although he still wished to extend his lands further, if this could be done easily. In particular, he had designs on the Polish province of West Prussia. Its acquisition would link East Prussia with the rest of his state and remove one of Prussia's geographical weaknesses. Another overriding aim was to prevent Austria recovering its former position, let alone its former land. All this needed to be done without recourse to war if at all possible. Frederick was well aware that Prussia had been lucky to survive the Seven Years War, and he had no wish to risk all his gains by getting involved in another major armed struggle. To retain and even increase his lands and power without fighting a war would require all of Frederick's talents.

Maria Theresa's aims were not dissimilar to Frederick's. She still hoped one day to regain Silesia, but, like Frederick, had no wish to fight further wars with him. She too had become only too well aware of the heavy price, both human and financial, which wars had already cost her state. However, she still deeply distrusted Frederick and was vigilant to resist any attempt on his part to further extend his lands or influence. But she had no wish to copy Frederick and his methods, and opposed on principle annexations of land based solely on the wish to increase state power. Her chief advisers on foreign policy, Kaunitz and her son Joseph, both favoured a more aggressive policy – confrontation with Frederick in Germany and conquest elsewhere. The result was that Austrian foreign policy after 1763 was a mixture of caution and recklessness.

Given the rivalries and suspicions of Prussia and Austria, the possibility of a further major war between them remained high. This prospect was far more worrying for Frederick than it was for Maria Theresa. Prussia was not merely bankrupt and exhausted, but had no allies in Europe. Great Britain had abandoned her in 1762 and, although there were informal negotiations in the following years, the alliance was never renewed. British leaders now saw their future being based on their colonial empire and did not intend any longer to become involved in disputes on the mainland of Europe. Austria, on the other hand, had retained its friendship with France, despite the evidence that neither side had benefited from the alliance during the Seven Years War. To Frederick's dismay, the Franco-Austrian alliance even showed

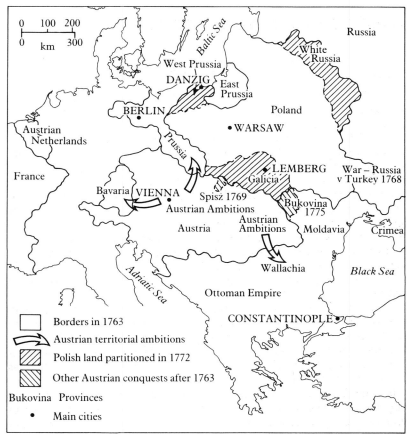

Prussian and Austrian foreign policy after 1763

signs of becoming firmer when Maria Theresa was able to arrange the marriage of her daughter, Marie-Antoinette, to the French *Dauphin* (heir to the throne), Louis. In the long run this marriage, thanks to Marie-Antoinette's frivolity and extravagance, was to damage both the alliance and the reputation of the French royal family. However, at the time Frederick could be forgiven for seeing it as evidence that Maria Theresa was again busy attempting to create a potential coalition against him.

In fact Frederick was wrong. The alliance was retained as a defensive move, to prevent a possible reconciliation between France and Prussia. The French government similarly had no further designs on Prussia.

Both Choiseul and Vergennes, who between them dominated French foreign policy after 1763, had decided to concentrate their resources on challenging Great Britain, the state which had emerged as the greatest threat to French power. France, like Britain, was turning its back on Europe, and the continuing alliance with Austria was designed for protection and not for any aggressive purposes.

2 The Prusso-Russian Alliance

Frederick, unaware that he had nothing to fear from Austria, looked for an ally to act as a counter to Austria's continuing alliance with France. He found such an ally in Russia, the state which had only recently been his most dangerous enemy. The new ruler of Russia, the Tsarina Catherine II (1762–96) would eventually prove to be a successful and skilful conquerer and one who, like Frederick, gained the title of 'the Great'. But in 1763 she had only recently come to the throne. At this stage her chief concern was with her neighbour Poland. This large but weak state enjoyed the doubtful privilege of having an elected monarch. The previous king, Augustus III, who had been prepared to follow Russian orders, had died in 1763. Catherine was anxious to have another pro-Russian monarch elected in his place. Her chosen candidate was a minor Polish nobleman, Stanislas Poniatowski. As a native Pole he might be more acceptable to his countrymen than another German prince such as Augustus. He could be expected to show appropriate gratitude and loyalty to the Tsarina who had plucked him from obscurity to make him king. The fact that Stanislas and Catherine had been lovers completed the bond.

To force such an obvious Russian puppet as the lover of the Tsarina onto the throne of Poland would doubtless bring protests from Poland's other neighbours, Austria and Prussia. Catherine required the support of one of these states if her plan was to succeed. She therefore was able to offer Frederick a mutually advantageous deal. If he would support Stanislas Poniatowski's bid to become King of Poland, Catherine would in return offer a defensive alliance. Russia would support Prussia with troops and/or money if Frederick was ever attacked by another state, and Frederick would do the same for Catherine. The alliance was signed in 1764 and Stanislas Poniatowski was, with the help of some heavy Russian bribes, duly elected as King of Poland.

Catherine was well pleased with the arrangement. She had secured the friendship of the most feared king and army in Europe and had installed her client as King of Poland without having to fight a war in order to achieve it. This was in marked contrast to the installation of the previous King of Poland, which had only been achieved after a six-year war (see pages 40–1). For Frederick the situation was more complicated. To be sure, he had secured the ally he needed, and he felt, not unreasonably, that it was this alliance which acted as a deterrent to

Maria Theresa making another attempt to reconquer Silesia. On the other hand, he was not sure that he was wise to help Russia to expand into Poland. In his *Political Testament* of 1768 he expressed great fears about the rise of Russian power, writing 'how insane and blind Europe is, that she contributes to the rise of a people which may some day become her own doom'. He feared that they were 'unassailable' and wrote that he feared the Russian army 'more than he feared God'. He predicted that one day Prussia might have to lead an alliance to stem the Russian flood. Yet this same Frederick could also express delight at having used Russian power to his own advantage, and he was only too pleased to renew the alliance in 1772. Clearly he felt that the short-term advantages of the alliance outweighed the longer-term risks.

Frederick hoped that he would never need to come to the aid of his new ally. He wrote that 'the best thing is that there are grounds for assuming the alliance will never be invoked: otherwise I would have been very foolish to let myself in for all this'. He expected, in short, to get all the benefits of the alliance, without having to pay the price for it.

It is too simple to see this alliance as just another example of Frederick's Machiavellian exploitation of other countries. In fact it represented a change of policy for him. Whilst all his previous alliances had been temporary wartime arrangements against an enemy, this one was designed as a permanent peacetime alliance to help avoid a war. The idea of defensive alliances to deter aggressors is one which has been common in Europe during the last hundred years, but at this time it was relatively new. Frederick, the master of warfare, was now initiating a new type of foreign policy, which would give Eastern Europe a period of much-needed stability. From now on, diplomacy rather than war would be the main weapon used by Frederick to increase the power of his state.

3 The First Partition of Poland

In 1768 war broke out between Russia and the Ottoman Empire. This war, in a distant corner of Europe (see the map on page 129) appeared at first to be of little interest to either Austria or Prussia. However, when in 1770 the Russian armies were threatening to conquer large areas of the Balkans (present day Romania), Austria became seriously alarmed. Such conquests would mean that a weak Ottoman neighbour would be replaced by a powerful Russia – a state which was, moreover, allied to Austria's greatest enemy. Austria was threatened with encirclement by enemies. In addition, Russia was conquering lands which Austria had long seen as her sphere of influence. Kaunitz had for some time been urging Maria Theresa to conquer some territory in the Balkans as compensation for the loss of Silesia. Now it appeared Russia would get the land first.

When the Russians refused to pull back from their conquests,

Austria agreed to assist the Turks. When news of these negotiations reached Berlin, Frederick became seriously alarmed. If Austria did go to war against Russia, Catherine would expect Frederick to fulfil the terms of the alliance and support her with his army. The last thing that Prussia needed in 1770 was another war, and he particularly had no wish to be involved in a war over land in the Balkans which was of no interest to Prussia. It was at this stage that Frederick suggested an alternative to a damaging war in Eastern Europe which nobody really wanted. Russia would be asked to limit her conquests in the Balkans, but as compensation would be given a large portion of Polish land. The Russian threat to Austria would be eliminated without a war, and Austria would also receive some Polish land as compensation. Finally, Prussia would help herself to West Prussia as her share of the spoils, and to ensure that the balance of power between the three major eastern states was maintained. Complicated negotiations lasting many months followed, and it was not until 1772 that agreement was reached. The First Partition of Poland, imposed on a state too weak to defend itself, resulted in sizeable acquisitions for each of three robbers.

There is no doubt that Frederick was the prime mover of the idea to partition Poland. The First Partition was an act of aggression comparable to his attack on Silesia in 1740. The interests of the state outweighed any moral considerations. By the standards of the eighteenth century, however, Frederick had done nothing wrong. On the contrary, contemporary opinion blamed Poland for its own fate. If it had not been so weak and helpless, it would not have been a temptation to its neighbours. Frederick was pleased with the Partition not just because it avoided a disastrous war. The province acquired, West Prussia, was relatively small but extremely useful. It linked East Prussia with Brandenburg, thereby consolidating Frederick's territories. Moreover the land and its 600,000 inhabitants had considerable economic potential, and in the years that followed Frederick devoted much energy to developing the area. All this had been achieved without a war and whilst maintaining the precious alliance with Russia. Frederick had shown he was as much master of the diplomatic chess board as he was on the battlefield.

When the proposal for partition was first put forward, Maria Theresa had rejected it out of hand. There were, however, powerful voices in favour of such an arrangement. Maria Theresa's son Joseph was now taking an increasing role in foreign affairs, and he argued strongly for participation. He was supported by Chancellor Kaunitz, and together they pressed the benefits of partition on their reluctant empress. The Austrian share, Galicia, which included the major city of Lvov (Lemberg), would be excellent compensation for the loss of Silesia. Catherine was willing to moderate her demands on the Ottoman Empire as part of the arrangement, and this would secure Austria's interests in the Balkans. It would avoid the necessity of a war that

Austria could not afford. Finally, Joseph argued, if Austria refused to participate in this robbery, then Prussia and Russia would partition Poland without their help, leaving Austria weaker than ever. All these were cogent arguments, based on the same principles of *raison d'état* that Frederick used. They came up against Maria Theresa's fundamental objection. She argued in a series of letters to Kaunitz and Joseph that what was being proposed was wrong, and that she could not, on principle, participate in such a crime.

1 We have been behaving like Prussians whilst trying to pretend we are honest . . . we have always tried to follow truth and justice, to honour our word and fulfil our obligations. This gained for us the admiration of Europe and the respect of our enemies. All this we
5 are now going to lose. I tell you that I do not know how to bear this, that nothing in the world has hurt me more than the loss of our good name . . . We must reject as evil and corrupting the idea of fishing for advantage in this whirlpool.
What right have we to rob an innocent nation? I do not
10 understand the policy whereby for the sake of convenience and advantage, we are obliged to imitate the wickedness of two others who are destroying an innocent power . . . A prince has no more justification than a private person for such behaviour . . . This would be a denial of everything we have done for thirty years. Let
15 us rather seek to stop the crimes of others. It is better to be considered weak than dishonest.

These desperate pleas had no effect, and it is significant that Maria Theresa's power had waned to the point where her views could be overruled. Frederick was cynical about the fact that Maria Theresa, who objected so strongly to Partition, ended up with the largest slice, commenting that 'she weeps, but she takes'. This verdict, although widely shared by historians, is perhaps harsh. Maria Theresa had been genuine in her opposition to Partition on principle. Joseph and Kaunitz were chiefly responsible both for Austrian participation, and for the extent of the claim.

Austria's active involvement in the First Partition indicate that in Austria as well as Prussia the interests of the state took precedence over legal or moral considerations. Having been beaten so often by Frederick, Joseph and Kaunitz were now copying his methods. For these reasons, Austria bears as much responsibility as Prussia for the Partition of Poland.

4 The War of Bavarian Succession

Despite two friendly meetings between Frederick and Joseph, in 1769 and 1770, and the co-operation between Austria and Prussia over the

First Partition of Poland, the basic mistrust between the two states continued. Frederick was particularly worried about the increasing influence Joseph exercised over Austrian foreign policy. Joseph reminded Frederick of what he had been like as a young ruler. He was ambitious, aggressive and unpredictable. What was clear was Joseph's determination to reassert Austrian primacy within the Holy Roman Empire. He took his responsibilities as Holy Roman Emperor seriously and tried, without success, to revive some of the legal rights formerly enjoyed by the emperors. Frederick was determined to maintain the balance of power established between Austria and Prussia in 1763. That he was both willing and able to maintain this balance was demonstrated in his last war, the War of Bavarian Succession of 1778–9.

In 1777 Elector Maximilian Joseph of Bavaria died childless, leaving his state to his nearest male relative, Karl Theodore, the ruler of the Palatine, Julich and Berg. Karl Theodore was uninterested in Bavaria and was willing to listen to Joseph's suggestion that he exchange Bavaria for the Austrian Netherlands. A triumphant Joseph was able to send Austrian troops into Bavaria in 1778.

There were obvious advantages for both rulers in this exchange of territories. By adding the Netherlands to his existing lands, Karl Theodore would create a power base in northern Europe. For Joseph, the acquisition of Bavaria would both round off Austrian lands, increase his influence in Germany and be effective compensation for the loss of Silesia. The Netherlands, a non-German province geographically separate from the rest of the Empire, would not matter in comparison. Joseph was pleased with his quick action which, he felt sure, would prevent any Prussian protests. 'The King of Prussia', he wrote, 'will not risk acting alone. The whole affair, if I am not mistaken, will pass off quietly'. Since he was taking over Bavaria with the consent of its ruler, there could be no possible objections.

Frederick had no intention of allowing an increase in Austrian power in Germany. He was uninterested in Bavaria as such, but saw that this was a challenge he could not ignore. Frederick wrote to his brother, Henry, that:

1 I know that these princes of the Empire are a collection of
  wretched nonentities, and I have no intention of becoming their
  Don Quixote; but if we let Austria exercise despotic power within
  Germany, we provide her with arms for use against ourselves. I
5 regard war as unavoidable. The Emperor wants it and his armies
  are massing.

Frederick was lucky that Karl Theodore had not seen fit to consult his heir, Duke Charles of Zweibrucken, before signing the treaty with Austria. Duke Charles, who wished to retain his claim to Bavaria, took his case to the Imperial Diet. When Frederick threatened to go to war on Duke Charles's behalf as a result of his plea to the Diet, Joseph was convinced it was a bluff and refused to negotiate, writing a letter to Frederick designed to insult him.

1 I hope you will kindly allow me, as head of the empire, some knowledge of our constitution. I do not believe that Your Majesty will expect Austria to submit to the Elector of Brandenburg in a case where he has no other authority.

5 It seems to me that you remember too much that you were a successful general, that you have an army of 200,000 men and a colonel who has written books on military history. God has given this advantage to other powers besides Prussia. If it gives Your Majesty pleasure to lead 200,000 men into battle, then I shall be

10 there with the same number, and I am ready to satisfy your passion for fighting. When we have fought and shown Europe a spectacle of obstinacy, we will return our swords into our scabbard.

Frederick had not been bluffing, and both sides were now in a position from which they could not retreat with dignity. In July 1778 Prussia declared war and, not for the first time, Prussian troops crossed the border into Bohemia.

The war proved to be a disappointment. The Prussian army had lost much of its quality since 1763. No battles were fought. Instead, a series of intricate manoeuvres led to deadlock in Bohemia. The Prussian troops proved to be much less reliable than in the old days, and 30,000 men deserted. Most of the rival armies' time was spent foraging for food, giving the war its derisory nickname of 'The Potato War'. By October 1778 the Prussian army had returned home and both sides were ready to start peace negotiations. If Frederick had been disappointed not to win any victories in this war, so too had Joseph. He too had dreamed of being a brilliant general and had hoped to emulate Frederick's early career in this campaign. The war showed that his military talents were no greater than those of his father.

The war also showed that neither side could rely on their nominal allies. Russia refused to send troops to help Frederick, whilst France similarly failed to assist Austria. This was a clear indication that these allies would only become involved in a war which served their own interests. However, both Russia and France were willing to act as mediators at the peace conference which opened in Teschen. The negotiations were made easier by Frederick's awareness that Maria Theresa was totally opposed to the war. She had taken the extraordinary step of writing a private letter to Frederick soon after it began assuring him that she had no wish to fight him and that she would be willing to accept a compromise.

The Treaty of Teschen (May 1779) gave Austria a small part of

Bavaria known as the Inn Quarter. The rest of Bavaria went to Karl Theodore and would pass on his death to the Duke of Zweibrucken. In addition, Austria agreed that the two small provinces of Ansbach and Bayreuth near Bavaria would go to Prussia when their current ruler, a distant relative of Frederick, died. Frederick could be well pleased with his achievement. Although his army had performed poorly, it had done enough to prevent Joseph acquiring significantly more land and power in Germany, and to demonstrate once again that nothing of importance could happen in the Holy Roman Empire without Prussian consent.

5 The Switch of Alliances

Despite his success in the War of Bavarian Succession, Frederick's last years continued to be dominated by fears about Austria. The failure of his ally, Russia, actively to support him in 1778 was an ominous indication that Catherine no longer cared about staying on good terms with Prussia. Over the years Frederick had come to depend on the alliance as his main deterrent against Austria. Catherine, by contrast, felt that the alliance was no longer of much value to Russia. Her main interest lay in conquering more land from the Ottoman Empire. Catherine, ever a cautious ruler reluctant to fight more enemies than she had to, set out to woo Joseph. Her aim was to persuade him to co-operate with her in a war against the Ottoman Empire. Together they could partition the Turkish lands in Europe and recreate a Christian kingdom in Constantinople. Kaunitz had long favoured a war against the Ottoman Empire and found little difficulty in persuading Joseph that here, rather than in Germany, could be found the land, glory and compensation for the loss of Silesia which he sought. There were, of course practical worries about an alliance with Russia. There was no doubt that Russia intended using Austria as a convenient means to extend her own power. Joseph, like Frederick, had reservations about making friends with such a powerful and potentially threatening neighbour. However, all these were minor disadvantages when compared to the huge benefits of not only conquering Turkish land, but having Russia as an ally, leaving Prussia once more isolated and friendless.

The switch in alliances took some time to bring about. The Russo-Prussian alliance was not renewed in 1781, but a further three years passed before the Russo-Austrian alliance was ratified, and not until 1788 that the long-awaited joint attack on the Ottoman Empire took place. Frederick had been in no position to compete with Joseph's offer of assistance in a war against the Ottoman Empire and once again found himself isolated. It was in this, apparently vulnerable, position that Frederick faced his last challenge from Joseph.

Frederick II (right) and other members of the League of Princes, 1785

6 The League of Princes, 1785

In 1785 Joseph felt confident enough to revive the scheme to exchange Bavaria for the Netherlands. This time the Duke of Zweibrucken's objections would be catered for with a bribe of one million guilders. For a second time Joseph hoped to present Frederick with a *fait accompli*, but on this occasion with Austria in a much stronger position than in 1778. However, Frederick proved again to be more than a match for the Austrian Emperor. Unable to find any allies amongst the European powers, he turned instead to the small German states who felt threatened by Habsburg ambitions. In July 1785 he became head of a League of German Princes, usually known as the *Fürstenbund*. The aim of the Union was 'the preservation and strengthening of the German Imperial system'. Within a few weeks, 14 of the leading states of Germany had joined the Union. The members included both Catholic and Protestant rulers and four of the seven Electors who chose the Holy Roman Emperor. It was a formidable vote of no confidence in Joseph. Joseph was now faced with a possible war against most of Germany if he persisted in the Bavarian exchange scheme. Both Russia and France made it clear that they would give no practical help to their nominal ally. Once again Joseph was obliged to drop the Bavarian scheme, this time for good.

Frederick could congratulate himself in his last months that even without Great Power allies he was able to defeat Austrian ambitions and retain Prussia's status as Austria's equal inside the Holy Roman Empire. There is, of course, some irony in the fact that Frederick, who started his career with unprovoked aggression against a new, weak and inexperienced monarch, and who had not hesitated to conquer and ravage a helpless Saxony in 1756, should now pose as the defender of the liberties of small German states. Once the *Fürstenbund* had achieved its aim of frustrating Austrian ambitions, Frederick ended its existence. It had been used purely to protect Prussian interests and not, as some nineteenth century German historians asserted, because Frederick favoured the eventual unification of Germany. It says much for Frederick's skill after 1763 that he was able to persuade so many small states that he had no wish to further increase his lands and that their best interests lay in having him as their protector against Austrian aggression. It was a fitting end to Frederick's brilliant career in war and diplomacy.

7 The Austrian Achievement

a) The Survival of a Great Power

Joseph's unexceptional performance in foreign policy between 1778 and 1785 appears on the surface to be the culmination of sixty years of Austrian decline. His reputation was to be further diminished by the dismal performance of the Austrian army when he did finally go to war against the Ottoman Empire in 1788. Whilst Catherine's army won a series of victories, the Austrian army was humiliatingly defeated. Austria was obliged to drop out of the war quickly and was lucky not to lose any land in the peace treaty. A defeat at the hands of the Turks had signalled the first clear evidence of Austrian decline in 1739. Fifty years later it seemed that history had repeated itself.

However, Austria's military decline was more apparent than real. The army, which had already shown some indications of improved quality during the Seven Years War, had performed no worse than the vaunted Prussian army in the Potato War. There were indications that whilst the Prussian army was becoming ossified by its rigid adherence to the increasingly outdated methods of Frederick, the Austrian army was showing some flexibility and an ability to adapt to new methods and weapons. During the wars against the French Revolution and Napoleon (1792–1815) the Austrian army fought much better than its Prussian counterpart. Austria, unlike Prussia, was never conquered (although she was defeated) by Napoleon, and in 1815 Austria had clearly emerged as the stronger of the two German states.

The Habsburgs had for centuries been faced with unique responsibilities and problems as rulers of Austria. They naturally expected to defend their own scattered and multi-national territories from rival Great Powers, but in addition they felt obliged to maintain primacy over the Holy Roman Empire, to defend the Catholic faith and to act as Europe's bastion against the threat from Turkey. Charles VI had conspicuously failed to cope with the demands of such a complex European-wide foreign policy, but Kaunitz could claim some success. He was able to reduce the Prussian threat by forming alliances with other powers, and at the same time acquired some land. Galicia (1772), Bukovina (1775) and the Inn Quarter (1779) together represented some compensation for the loss of Silesia and did something to restore Austrian prestige.

However, Kaunitz's success should not be overrated. Austria did not regain Silesia or its former position of unchallenged supremacy in Germany. Frederick continued to outmanoeuvre and humiliate the Austrians right up to his death. Although it is therefore possible to portray Kaunitz as a brilliant diplomat who restored Austrian prestige after the disasters of 1741, ending up with sizeable conquests and the centre of a system of diplomatic alliances, it is equally possible to see him as the man who failed to restore Austria's lands and who was responsible for Austria's inability to match Frederick's successful diplomacy.

b) The Making of the Austrian State

Edward Crankshaw, in his history of the Austrian Empire, gave his chapter on Maria Theresa the title 'The Making of Modern Austria'. This is a bold claim, but one which is probably justified. Charles VI had proved to be an honourable but mediocre ruler, who had surrounded himself with flatterers and who had no understanding of the limits to either his power or his finances. Under his benign rule, Austria lost wars and went bankrupt. No attempt was made to strengthen government institutions, and real power remained with the nobles, the estates and the Church. Austria under Charles VI had the dubious distinction of sharing the same problems as Poland. Faced with the skill and aggressiveness of Frederick II, it is not impossible that Austria could have shared Poland's fate.

That this did not happen was not entirely due to Maria Theresa. Frederick himself must take some credit for Austria's survival as a state after 1740. He had no wish to see Austria broken up entirely. Austria had for centuries prevented France from controlling the Holy Roman Empire, and any collapse of the Austrian Empire might lead to a revival of French ambitions. He preferred to see a weak Austria to a resurgent France as his neighbour, and accordingly acted throughout the War of Austrian Succession to ensure that Austria survived. Twice he signed peace treaties with Austria and dropped out of the war at crucial times to help ensure that Austria was in a position to defeat the French.

Despite this, most of the credit for the survival of Austria remains due to Maria Theresa. Prussian aggression obliged her to tackle some of the problems of her state. Unlike Joseph, she had no clear vision of a unitary centralised Austrian autocratic state, but she did see that certain reforms were essential if the state was to survive. Her lack of a clear vision was both her weakness and her strength. It was a weakness in that her reforms were often unco-ordinated, and that where she held strong personal views these prevailed over the need for reform. She continued to put her faith in the Catholic Church and to persecute her substantial religious minorities where a clear-headed vision of state power would have led her to reduce such divisions in her state. She continued her father's extravagance, building palaces and leading a life at court which aroused admiration but created bankruptcy. She showed excessive loyalty to her husband. Finally she proved to be a most cautious reformer who avoided tackling problems, as in Hungary, where to do so might provoke opposition.

Nevertheless Austria owed much to Maria Theresa. Her policies were pragmatic and realistic. She was cautious and willing to compromise. A more radical approach to reform, such as that advocated by her son, might have aroused much stronger opposition. Whilst it is untrue to claim, as Macartney does, that there were 'no serious revolts' during her reign, the revolts that did take place (most notably that of the Bohemian serfs) were contained and were never widespread enough to threaten the government. Maria Theresa showed common sense in deciding what was realistic and achievable, and considerable skill in choosing her advisers and ministers. She was aware that her first priority must be to reduce the powers of the nobles whilst creating an efficient system of government and an honest civil service. She showed more concern than Frederick for the welfare of her people and had a strong sense of her responsibilities. She treated her people as she treated her own family, once even describing herself as the 'mother of her people'. When she died there was evidence of genuine mourning amongst her people, although this may have been as much to do with fears of what her erratic son might do without her restraining influence as real affection for their monarch.

8 The Prussian Achievement

Prussia in 1713 had suffered from many of the same weaknesses as Austria. Here too was a state with a backward economy and scattered territories which made it very vulnerable to attack. Prussia as well as Austria suffered from powerful nobles and a monarch whose power was absolute only in theory. It was the joint achievement of Frederick William I and Frederick II to weld the scattered provinces into a unitary state, to turn Prussia into one of the great powers of Europe and to create a system of government and an army which, on the surface at least, was second to none in Europe.

It was Frederick William who deserves most of the credit for the creation of the Prussian state. Whilst his son did add some new elements, notably a sweeping law reform which far exceeded Maria Theresa's very modest efforts in Austria, the provision of state granaries to prevent starvation, and a vigorous if limited attempt to develop Prussian trade and industry, the creation of the state which allowed these developments was the achievement of Frederick William. Frederick II proved to be cautious to the point of conservativism when it came to reforming the system of government he inherited. The General Directory, the endless tours of inspection and the structure of the armed forces were all retained, even when it was obvious that they had outlived their usefulness. Frederick was in fact far less innovative and reforming than Maria Theresa. By the end of his reign his system was no longer significantly superior to its Austrian counterpart as it had been in 1740, and events after 1790 were to prove that Austria was much better able to adapt to the challenge of Napoleon.

If Frederick II can be criticised for not improving his father's system of government, there were areas in which he showed greater skill and understanding than Maria Theresa. Frederick, who had no strong religious convictions of his own, continued his father's policies of religious toleration for all groups, so avoiding one of the chief sources of division within the Austrian Empire. Frederick also demonstrated a different approach to Maria Theresa in his dealings with the nobles. Rather than trying to exclude them from power, he entered into partnership with them, flattering them and granting them a virtual monopoly of senior positions in both government and the army. This made Frederick to a certain extent dependent on the nobles, but it was probably a more realistic way to govern his lands effectively than Maria Theresa's reliance on a small group of largely middle-class bureaucrats. Finally, Frederick had a keen awareness of the necessity for financial solvency. Maria Theresa's extravagence at court meant that she continued to depend on loans from her nobles to keep her government afloat. Frederick by contrast could afford to enter a partnership with the nobles, confident that he would never become excessively dependent on them.

Frederick William and Frederick II had created a state which was ultimately based on the army for its survival. It is this which, above all, distinguishes Prussia from Austria. Even after all of Frederick's successes, Prussia remained a first-class power based on second-class resources. Prussian power was fragile, and the events of 1806 demonstrated how quickly it could be broken. Nevertheless, the achievements of Frederick William and Frederick II had been remarkable. They had created the most efficient system of government and the finest army in Europe. They also left a significant legacy for the future history of Germany.

9 Habsburg-Hohenzollern Rivalry and Europe

For centuries it had been taken for granted that Austria was the dominant state within Germany and that the main threats to her position came from the external threats of the Ottoman Empire and France. The unexpected challenge from Prussia, coming as it did at a time when both France and the Ottoman Empire were in decline, transformed the politics, not just of Germany, but of Europe as a whole. An exhausting series of wars left both states broadly similar in strength and influence. In 1786 Austria remained the larger of the two states with an (apparently) enviable position in the centre of an alliance system. Prussia was, however, well able to hold its own with a combination of diplomatic skill and the reputation of the greatest captain and army of the eighteenth century.

The conflict between the two states probably weakened them both and Germany as a whole in the long run. It certainly made it easier for Catherine II in Russia to expand her territories by playing off against each other the only two powers which could have prevented her conquests. Whilst Catherine showed some skill in allying first with Prussia and then with Austria as suited her circumstances, it must be recognised that the deep mutual suspicions between the two German states made her task much easier. Similarly, Austro-Prussian hostility even after 1790 prevented them from combining against the threat of the French Revolution and considerably eased Napoleon's work when he found that he only had to fight one of the German powers at a time.

The history of Austria in the eighteenth century offers a good example of the dangers when a once powerful state allows its authority to rest mainly on its reputation. The rise of Prussia and its successful challenge to Austria's authority remains one of the very few examples in history when a small state with modest resources has successfully joined the ranks of the great powers and changed the balance of power. This proved to be a fragile and short-lived success; it was a remarkable achievement nonetheless, and one for which Frederick William and Frederick II share the credit.

1764–1781

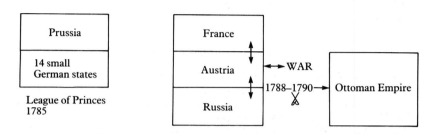

1781–1790

Summary – Austria and Prussia after 1763

Making notes on 'Austria and Prussia after 1763'

It is unlikely that you will be asked a question solely on Austro-Prussian relations after 1763 in the examination. It is therefore important that you see your notes on this chapter as carrying on from those you have made on the years 1740–63. The main features of this period you need to have clear notes on are:

1 What were Prussia's aims in foreign policy after 1763?
2 What were Austria's aims in foreign policy after 1763?
3 What methods did Prussia use to try to achieve these aims?
4 What methods did Austria use to try to achieve her aims?
5 Did Frederick achieve his aims after 1763?
6 Did Austria achieve its aims after 1763?
7 What were the effects of Austro-Prussian rivalry?

You should be able to build up a useful set of notes by using these headings and by referring to the appropriate headings in this chapter.

Source-based questions on 'Austria and Prussia after 1763'

1 Maria Theresa's views on the First Partition of Poland

Read the extracts from the letters of Maria Theresa on page 133 and then answer the following questions.

a) Explain the references to i) 'we have been behaving like Prussians' (line 1), ii) 'an innocent nation' (line 9), and iii) 'imitate the wickedness of two others' (line 11) (*6 marks*)

b) What evidence did Maria Theresa have for claiming that Austria's earlier policies had 'gained for us the admiration of Europe and the respect of our enemies' (lines 3–4)? (*4 marks*)

c) Explain why her argument that 'it is better to be thought weak than dishonest' was unacceptable to Joseph and Kaunitz (*4 marks*)

d) Does the evidence from Maria Theresa's foreign policy from 1740 onwards suggest that her policies were principled or hypocritical? (*6 marks*)

2 The War of Bavarian Succession

Read the letters from Frederick II on page 134 and Joseph II on page 135 and then answer the following questions.

a) Explain the references to i) 'Don Quixote' (page 134, line 3), ii) 'The Emperor' (page 134, line 5), and iii) 'The Elector of Brandenburg' (page 135, line 3) (*6 marks*)

b) Why did Frederick think that Austria's acquisition of Bavaria would 'provide her with arms for use against ourselves'? (*4 marks*)

c) In what ways was Joseph's letter designed to anger Frederick? (*4 marks*)

d) Comparing the tone and substance of Maria Theresa's letters on the Polish Partition (page 133) and Joseph's letter to Frederick. Was Frederick justified in feeling Joseph was a greater threat to Prussia than Maria Theresa? (*6 marks*)

3 Visual Sources of the Austro-Prussian Conflict

Look at the portraits of Frederick William I (page 32), Charles VI (page 17), Frederick II (page 118), Maria Theresa (page 100), and the cartoon on page 137.

a) Formal portraits of monarchs were commissioned by the rulers themselves and were designed to please the person portrayed. What image of the monarchs was being created by each of the four portraits? (*8 marks*)

b) How accurate, in each case, is the image presented by the portrait? (*8 marks*)

c) What value are such formal portraits to the historian? (*4 marks*)

d) Given that the meeting of princes shown in the cartoon never actually took place, of what use is the cartoon to historians? (*5 marks*)

Chronological Table

1618	Thirty Years War in Germany began
1648	Treaty of Westphalia ended Thirty Years War
1658	Leopold I elected Holy Roman Emperor
1683	Siege of Vienna by Ottoman Empire
1685	Charles VI of Austria born
1688–97	War of the League of Augsburg
1692	Hanover became the ninth Electorate of the Empire
1697	Augustus II of Saxony elected King of Poland
1699	Treaty of Karlowitz: Austria gained Hungary, Croatia, Transylvania and Slovenia from the Ottoman Empire
1700	War of Spanish Succession began
1701	Frederick III became King Frederick I of Prussia
1703–11	Charles supported by the allies as King of Spain
1703–11	Hungarian revolt against Austrian rule
1704	August, Battle of Blenheim
1705	Joseph I elected Holy Roman Emperor
1711	April, Joseph I died. Charles VI became ruler of Austria
1712	January, Frederick II of Prussia born
1713	Charles VI introduced the Pragmatic Sanction
	February, Frederick William I became King of Prussia
	April, Treaty of Utrecht ended War of Spanish Succession
1714	March, Treaty of Rastdat between France and Austria ended their involvement in the War of Spanish Succession
	August, Elector George of Hanover became King George I of England
1715	Prussia joined Great Northern War against Sweden
1715	Louis XV became King of France
1716	War between Austria and Ottoman Empire began
1717	Prussian education decree
	May, Maria Theresa of Austria born
1718	July, Treaty of Passarowitz: Austria gained Wallachia and Serbia from Ottoman Empire
1718–19	War between Austria and Spain
1720	February, Peace made between Prussia and Sweden. Prussia gained Stettin
1723	Establishment of General Directory in Prussia
1726	Austro-Russian alliance
1729	Prussia accepted Pragmatic Sanction
1733	Establishment of canton system for army recruitment in Prussia
	February, death of Augustus II of Poland
	August, War of Polish Succession began

1736	Austro-Turkish War began
1738	November, Treaty of Vienna ended War of Polish Succession: Augustus III confirmed as King of Poland, Stanislas Lesczinski became Duke of Lorraine and Francis of Lorraine married Maria Theresa of Austria
1739	July, Battle of Crocyka: Ottoman army defeated Austria
	September, Treaty of Belgrade ended Austro-Turkish War: Austria lost Wallachia and Serbia
	October, War of Jenkins' Ear between Great Britain and Spain began
1740	31 May, Frederick William died: Frederick II became King of Prussia
	20 October, Charles VI died: Maria Theresa became ruler of Austria
	16 December, Prussia invaded Silesia
1741	April, Battle of Mollwitz: Frederick II defeated Austria and kept Silesia
	May–July: France, Spain, Bavaria and Saxony joined war against Austria: start of War of Austrian Succession
	June: Diet of Pressburg: Maria Theresa appealed for help from Hungary
	August, French army invaded Bohemia
1742	January: Charles VI, Elector of Bavaria, elected Holy Roman Emperor
	May, Battle of Chotusitz: Prussian victory over Austria
	July, Treaty of Berlin between Prussia and Austria
	December, French driven from Bohemia
1743	June, Battle of Dettingen: British defeated the French
	June, Bavaria conquered by Austria
1744	August, Frederick II invaded Saxony: start of Second Silesian War
1745	June, Battle of Hohenfriedburg: Prussian victory over Austria
	September, Francis, husband of Maria Theresa, elected Holy Roman Emperor
	September, Battle of Soor: Prussian victory over Austria
	December, Treaty of Dresden: Prussia retained Silesia and accepted Francis I as Holy Roman Emperor
1747	Maria Theresa accepted Haugwitz's tax reform plans
1748	Supreme Office of Justice established in Austria
	October, Treaty of Aix-la-Chapelle (Aachen) between France and Austria ended War of Austrian Succession
1749	Austrian and Bohemian Chancelleries combined
1750	Kaunitz appointed Austrian Ambassador to France
1753	Kaunitz became Chancellor of Austria
	Maria Theresa set up Commission on Law Reform

	Maria Theresa established Directories of Commerce and Foreign Affairs
1756	January, Convention of Westminster between Prussia and Britain
	1 May, First Treaty of Versailles between Austria and France
	17 May, Britain declared war on France
	29 August, Frederick II attacked Saxony: start of Seven Years War
1757	January, Holy Roman Empire declared war on Prussia. Plan for partition of Prussia drawn up
	February, Russia declared war on Prussia
	March, Sweden declared war on Prussia
	1 May, Second Treaty of Versailles between Austria and France. France declared war on Prussia
	6 May, Battle of Prague: Austrian army defeated by Frederick II
	18 June, Battle of Kolin: Prussians defeated
	5 November, Battle of Rossbach: Frederick II heavily defeated French
	5 December, Battle of Leuthen: Frederick II heavily defeated Austrians
1758	April, start of British subsidies to Prussia
	April, Prussian invasion of Moravia
	25 August, Battle of Zorndorf: Frederick II defeated Russians
	14 October, Battle of Hochkirch: Austrians defeated Frederick II
1759	1 August, Battle of Minden: Hanoverians heavily defeated French
	12 August, Battle of Kunersdorf: Austrians and Russians heavily defeated Frederick II
1760	Council of State established in Austria
	15 August, Battle of Leignitz: Prussians defeated Austrians
	October, Russian army occupied Berlin for four days
	3 November, Battle of Torgau: Frederick II defeated Austrians
1761	October, fall of William Pitt's government in Great Britain led to the ending of British subsidies to Prussia
1762	5 January, death of Empress Elizabeth of Russia: accession of Peter III
	5 May, Russia signed peace treaty with Prussia
	17 July, Peter III assassinated: accession of Catherine II
1763	Prussian education decree
	10 February, Treaty of Paris ended Seven Years War between Britain, France and Spain

	15 February, Treaty of Hubertusburg ended Seven Years War between Austria and Prussia
	3 October, Augustus III of Poland died
1764	April, Prusso-Russian alliance signed
	7 September, Stanislas Poniatowski elected King of Poland
1765	Prussia established state bank
	18 August, death of Emperor Francis: Joseph II elected Holy Roman Emperor
1768–74	Russo-Turkish War
1769	February, Austria seized Spisz from Poland
1772	August, first Partition of Poland
1773	Austria expelled Jesuits
1774	Death of Louis XV: accession of Louis XVI
1775	Serious peasant revolt in Bohemia
	Austria annexed Bukovina from the Ottoman Empire
1776	Torture abolished in Austria
1777	Attempt by Maria Theresa to expel Jews from Vienna
	December, death of Elector Maximilian Joseph of Bavaria
1778	June, Austrian army occupied Bavaria
	3 July, Prussia declared war on Austria: start of the War of Bavarian Succession ('Potato War')
1779	13 May, Treaty of Teschen ended War of Bavarian Succession
1780	29 November, death of Maria Theresa: accession of Joseph II
1781	February, Austro-Russian alliance signed
1784	Austro-Russian alliance ratified
1785	January, Joseph II revived plan to exchange Bavaria for Netherlands
	23 July, Frederick created *Fürstenbund* (League of Princes) to resist Austria
1786	17 August, death of Frederick II: accession of Frederick William II
1788	February, Joseph II declared war on Turkey
1789	French Revolution began
1790	February, death of Joseph II: accession of Leopold II
1791	August, Austro-Turkish War ended
1792	Austro-Prussian alliance against France
1794	Reform of Prussian legal code completed
1797	Death of Frederick William II of Prussia: accession of Frederick William III
1806	14 October, Battle of Jena: Napoleon destroyed old Prussia
1815	Congress of Vienna ended Napoleonic wars and restored Austrian domination over Germany

Further Reading

1 Histories of Germany

There are a number of general histories of Germany in the eighteenth century which offer a useful survey of the Habsburg-Hohenzollern conflict. One of the most recent is:

J. Gagliardo, *Germany under the Old Regime* (Longman, 1991)
This covers our period in four chapters and offers a balanced view of all the main characters. The book is well-written, interesting and well researched. The bibliography is a useful place to start if you are attempting to locate the most helpful specialist books.

Much older, but reliable and packed with information is:

H. Holborn, *A History of Modern Germany, 1648–1840* (Eyre & Spottiswoode, 1965)
There are several good histories of Prussia. I particularly recommend:

H.W. Koch, *A History of Prussia* (Longman, 1978)
It is supported by a range of useful primary sources, and gives equal balance to domestic and foreign policy issues.

General histories of the Austrian Empire are harder to find:

E. Wangermann, *The Austrian Achievement* (Thames & Hudson, 1973)
This offers a competent and reliable survey of the period, and is probably the best book you are likely to find.

Lighter but more accessible is:

E. Crankshaw, *The Habsburgs* (Weidenfeld & Nicolson, 1971)
This offers sympathetic portraits of Charles VI and Maria Theresa and has attractive illustrations. However, it does not go into any great detail and is perhaps unduly kind to these monarchs.

2 Biographies

There is no biography of Charles VI in English, and the only biography of Frederick William I is now over fifty years old and difficult to get hold of. However, there is no shortage of biographies of Frederick II and Maria Theresa.

For Maria Theresa, the best biography remains:

E. Crankshaw, *Maria Theresa* (Longman, 1969)
This contains a range of primary sources. Crankshaw is sympathetic to

Maria Theresa and concludes that she achieved a great deal, but also accepts that she sometimes failed and made mistakes. It is rather better than its chief rival:

C. Macartney, *Maria Theresa and the House of Austria* (Lawrence Verry, 1969)
Macartney deals with domestic policies rather too briefly for your purposes.

Historians have always been attracted to the personality and achievements of Frederick II. There have therefore been many biographies about him. Two are more useful than the others:

L. Reiners, *Frederick the Great* (New English Library, 1978)
Reiners gives equal emphasis to his domestic and foreign policies. You should find this helpful, as long as you take into account the bias in favour of his subject. It is rather more interesting to read than:

D.B. Horn, *Frederick the Great and the Rise of Prussia* (English University Press, 1964)
However, Horn does have the advantage of discussing Frederick's impact on the later history of Germany.

3 Specialist studies

For those interested in finding out more about the Partitions of Poland and the wars against the Ottoman Empire, there is

A. Stiles, *Russia, Poland and the Ottoman Empire* (Hodder & Stoughton Access to History Series, 1991)
This offers a clear description of the causes and effects of the Partitions and analyses the Partitions from the Russian and Polish viewpoints.

A detailed analysis of Frederick's military campaigns and a strong argument for his military genius can be found in:

C. Duffy, *Frederick the Great: A Military Life* (Routledge, 1985)
This will be found heavy going by all but the most enthusiastic students of war.

H.M. Scott (Ed), *Enlightened Absolutism* (Macmillan, 1990)
Includes essays on Austria and Maria Theresa's policies towards Hungary.

The growing influence of Joseph on Maria Theresa's later policies is covered in detail in two books:

D. Beales, *Joseph II: Volume I* (Cambridge University Press, 1987)

This covers Joseph's early life in great detail. You may find it easier to read than:

T.C.W. Blanning, *Joseph II and Enlightened Despotism* (Longman, 1970)
Chapter 2 covers the reforms of Maria Theresa and Joseph's frustrating years of apprenticeship.

Index

Readers seeking a specific piece of information might find it helpful to consult the *Contents* and the *Chronological Table* as well as this brief *Index*.

Bavaria 4–6, 26, 29, 60–1, 135–9
Bohemia 15–16, 22–3, 60, 62, 72, 95–6, 136

Catherine II 77, 131, 133, 137, 143
Charles VI 6–7, 14–29, 33, 40–1, 55–6, 140
Cocceji 107–8, 115, 120

Daun 72, 74–6, 94–5

East Prussia 45, 72, 77
Elizabeth 67, 70, 75, 77
Eugene 11–14, 16, 20, 23, 26, 29, 41

France 3–6, 11–13, 26, 29, 36, 58–74, 77–9, 129–31, 136, 141
Francis of Lorraine 59, 63, 87, 94
Frederick I 5, 31, 33, 50
Frederick II 6–7, 28, 41, 44, 48–50, 55–82, 92, 101, 107–39, 141–3
Frederick William I 6–7, 31–50, 57, 59, 80, 122–4, 142–3
Frederick William II 120–1
Frederick William III 120–1

General Directory 42–4, 109
Great Britain 6, 14, 40, 60–1, 63–71, 73–4, 76–8, 81

Hanover 5, 67, 72–4
Haugwitz 89–92, 98
Holy Roman Empire 1–3, 25, 64, 70, 135, 139
Hungary 13, 16, 22–3, 24–5, 60, 91, 93

Joseph I 4, 14, 18–19
Joseph II 88, 97–103, 129, 133–9

Kaunitz 65–71, 74, 89–90, 98, 129, 132–4, 137, 140

Leopold I 4, 5, 11–14, 16, 22
Leopold of Anhalt-Dessau 31–2, 35, 38, 55
Louis XIV 3–4, 11, 15, 23
Louis XV 59, 64, 66–9, 71–3, 79
Maria Theresa 6–7, 24–9, 56–106, 129–42
Marlborough 4, 13, 47
Mercantalism 9, 22, 112–13

Napoleon 80, 118, 121, 140, 143

Ottoman Empire 11–12, 14, 22, 27, 132–3, 137, 139

Peter III, 75, 77
Poland 5, 40–1, 131–4
Pragmatic Sanction 20, 21, 24–9, 41

Russia 6, 27, 40, 56, 67, 70–2, 74–6, 78, 131–4, 136–7, 139

Saxony 5–6, 26–7, 60, 62–3, 69–70, 74–6, 78
Silesia 6, 55–65, 71–3, 75–6, 79, 114
Spain 14, 24, 60
Sweden 40, 58, 71–2

West Prussia 114, 129, 133